Cambridge Elements

Elements in the Philosophy of Immanuel Kant
edited by
Desmond Hogan
Princeton University
Howard Williams
University of Cardiff
Allen Wood
Indiana University

KANT ON SOCIAL SUFFERING

Nuria Sánchez Madrid
Complutense University of Madrid

Shaftesbury Road, Cambridge CB2 8EA, United Kingdom

One Liberty Plaza, 20th Floor, New York, NY 10006, USA

477 Williamstown Road, Port Melbourne, VIC 3207, Australia

314–321, 3rd Floor, Plot 3, Splendor Forum, Jasola District Centre, New Delhi – 110025, India

103 Penang Road, #05–06/07, Visioncrest Commercial, Singapore 238467

Cambridge University Press is part of Cambridge University Press & Assessment, a department of the University of Cambridge.

We share the University's mission to contribute to society through the pursuit of education, learning and research at the highest international levels of excellence.

www.cambridge.org
Information on this title: www.cambridge.org/9781009565776

DOI: 10.1017/9781009446457

© Nuria Sánchez Madrid 2025

This publication is in copyright. Subject to statutory exception and to the provisions of relevant collective licensing agreements, no reproduction of any part may take place without the written permission of Cambridge University Press & Assessment.

When citing this work, please include a reference to the DOI 10.1017/9781009446457

First published 2025

A catalogue record for this publication is available from the British Library

ISBN 978-1-009-56577-6 Hardback
ISBN 978-1-009-44644-0 Paperback
ISSN 2397-9461 (online)
ISSN 2514-3824 (print)

Cambridge University Press & Assessment has no responsibility for the persistence or accuracy of URLs for external or third-party internet websites referred to in this publication and does not guarantee that any content on such websites is, or will remain, accurate or appropriate.

For EU product safety concerns, contact us at Calle de José Abascal, 56, 1°, 28003 Madrid, Spain, or email eugpsr@cambridge.org

Kant on Social Suffering

Elements in the Philosophy of Immanuel Kant

DOI: 10.1017/9781009446457
First published online: July 2025

Nuria Sánchez Madrid
Complutense University of Madrid

Author for correspondence: Nuria Sánchez Madrid, nuriasma@ucm.es

Abstract: This Element analyses how Kant's practical philosophy approaches social suffering, while also taking into account the elusiveness of this concept in his work, especially when viewed through a contemporary lens. It claims that Kant's theory of human dignity is a vital tool for detecting social structures in need of improvement, even if the high demands it imposes on the subject show a propensity to conceal situations of domination and oppression. In his writings, Kant investigated various societal challenges such as widespread poverty, duties towards animals, care for the mentally ill, and motherhood out of wedlock, suggesting that the state should solve most of these through financial support from the wealthier segments of society. Although the direct testimony of victims of social suffering does not play a role in Kant's approach, the author holds that he views social interdependence – including, notably, non-humans – as a fundamental commitment underpinning human development.

This Element also has a video abstract:
www.cambridge.org/EPIK_Nuria_abstract

Keywords: social suffering, domination, oppression, exploitation, gender discrimination

© Nuria Sánchez Madrid 2025

ISBNs: 9781009565776 (HB), 9781009446440 (PB), 9781009446457 (OC)
ISSNs: 2397-9461 (online), 2514-3824 (print)

Contents

1 Introduction   1

2 Kant's Approach to Human Dignity: At the Cross-roads of Religion, Morals and Anthropology   5

3 Enlarging the Framework of Suffering: How to Treat Animals and the Mentally Ill Well?   22

4 Poverty Relief and Social Suffering   33

5 Kant on the Social Suffering of Women   44

6 Conclusions   55

   List of Abbreviations of Kant's Works   58

   Bibliography   60

1 Introduction

Kant's practical philosophy is not often noted for championing the alleviation of 'social suffering' (Kleinman, Das, and Lock 1997: ix; Wilkinson 2005: 9–12; Renault 2017: vi–ix), which can be understood as a violation of the basic rights and dignity of the human being. On the same token, Kant has often been criticized as an author not especially attuned to emotional accounts of the value of human existence. In fact, the priority of practical reason demands the human being subordinate the satisfaction of his individual human desires and interests to the fulfilment of the moral law, given that, in Kant's view, the emotions do not provide a reliable path to virtue. With this in mind, it is not surprising that Kant's philosophy does not directly address social suffering or consider the direct testimony of those suffering injustice.

Even with an awareness of this understandable reluctance to view Kant as an author useful for reflection on the causes and effects of social suffering, this Element aims to shed light on Kant's analyses of obstacles to the full development of the rational and moral potential embedded within every human being. I wish to stress that even though we cannot trace, in Kant's writings, a necessarily 'compassionate' approach, Kant does show an awareness that social interaction entails injustices and abuses that must be remedied in order to foster the growth of a lawful civil society. While it's true that he might have drawn more ambitious conclusions from this awareness, an appraisal of Kant's attitude towards issues such as poverty, animal suffering, mental illness, and the oppression of women will help to raw a more nuanced image of Kant's attention to social change. Importantly, my account does not discount the interconnection of Kant's moral theory with a 'bourgeois coldness' and a sadist attitude to fundamental human needs foregrounded by prominent theorists from the Frankfurt School as a specific trait of Kant's morality. On the contrary, I take this interpretation as a challenge to reveal some lesser known aspects of Kant's approach to the human experience of suffering, both in one's own person and in others In this vein, a well-known section of Adorno's *Negative Dialectics* stresses the repressive features of the main concepts of Kant's moral theory:

> All the concepts whereby the *Critique of Practical Reason* proposes, in honor of freedom, to fill the chasm between the Imperative and mankind—law, constraint, respect, duty—all of these are repressive. A causality produced by freedom corrupts freedom into obedience
>
> (Adorno 1973 [1966]: 232).

It's true that Kant himself promoted this rigorist image of human will in many of his writings. For instance, he claims in the *Groundwork of the Metaphysics of*

Morals that the beneficent agent, in fulfilling his duty, should have a 'temperament cold and indifferent to the sufferings of others, perhaps because he himself is provided with the special gift of patience and endurance toward his own sufferings and presupposes the same in every other or even requires it' (G 4: 398). This passage highlights a key issue in the *Groundwork*, as it identifies Christian values such as patience and composure as the psychological and moral dispositions required in order to cope with suffering. Consequently, this portrait of an ideal human agent, acting not through *self-interest*, but out of *respect* for the moral law, seems difficult to integrate with a society in which fellow citizens often need our help and where we often feel committed to relieve the burdens of others. Given these conditions, should the Kantian subject really behave coldly and indifferently towards the suffering of others?

It should be noted that in the aforementioned excerpt of the *Groundwork*, Kant seeks to distinguish between acting out of sympathy versus acting out of moral respect, rather than advocating for indifference towards others.[1] By highlighting this passage, I aim to show that Kant's moral theory does not relate the morality of a decision to an emotional reaction towards the suffering of others. At the same time, it is undeniable that Kant's practical philosophy encourages a duty of love towards other human beings, which includes beneficence, gratitude, and sympathy (DV § 29–35, 6: 452–458). Moreover, he advocates for cultivating the 'virtues of social intercourse' (DV § 48, 6: 473–474), insofar as he views these as useful in the sense that in some cases, one may 'fake it till they make it'. In fact, even if valued as mere aesthetical *parerga* of moral virtue, affability, sociability, and courtesy connect the subject with others and thus improve the quality of social interaction. In this context, it may be helpful to draw on Judith Shklar's invitation to ignore the question of attributing pain to the result of individual actions or external causes, instead simply providing help to those in need (1999: 126). As is well known, Kant places the moral value of human actions above their social and political consequences, which seems difficult to square with Shklar's view on alleviating social suffering. However, Kant seems to share some facets of Shklar's point of view in demanding that individual agents strive to alleviate the material scarcity and social vulnerability of others insofar as they may have been the beneficiaries of 'injustice of the government' or a 'general injustice' (DV § 31, 6: 454; Eth-Collins 27: 416).

This Element intends to explore whether Kant's writings address social suffering as a phenomenon deserving a conceptual appraisal.[2] The contemporary understanding of 'social suffering' primarily relates to damages resulting

---

[1] I am thankful to one of the reviewers of this Element for making me attentive to the context of this excerpt from *G* and suggesting me to nuance my original point about it.

[2] This Element focuses on *social suffering* and not merely on *human suffering* as an anthropological and psychological experience (Sen 2009; Levine 2009; Malpas and Lickiss 2012), as it attempts

from economic inequality, political and cultural oppression, or civil domination (Young 2011: 43–74). In contrast with this contemporary account of social suffering, Kant views women, dependent workers, animals, and those suffering from mental illness as unable to actively contribute to the commonwealth. Put differently, he does not consider the material benefits ensuing from the mentioned beings valuable enough to take them into account as co-legislators. This entails a blatant inconsistency with his republican account of the state and his moral theory, especially with the Formula of Humanity as an end in itself (G 4: 429). At the same time, however, he emphasizes that these individuals should not be abused or treated disrespectfully as a result. Of the groups mentioned, only male dependent workers could possibly 'work their way up' – to use a celebrated Kantian expression – to become active participants in society. Such a perspective towards vulnerable social agents does not, however, overshadow Kant's clear awareness of the state's duty to mitigate conducts that give rise to injustice. Consequently, I will trace how Kant's subtle account of *social suffering* underpins his understanding of *social justice*, a concept itself often difficult to define and as such one neglected by most Kantian scholars. This analysis will require parsing not only certain social dynamics involved in the various injustices the subject might experience, but also Kant's view that wealthy people must behave beneficently towards outcast individuals, put forth in his *Lectures on Ethics*. Such points confirm that Kant had quite an ambivalent attitude to social change: in the aforementioned lectures, he addresses individual agency as a tool for amending societal injustices, yet later, in the *Doctrine of Right*, he touts the agency of political institutions, establishing the foundation for political public authority.

Perhaps Kant's account of the Enlightenment and its emphasis on the role of individual social agents in influencing public beliefs and thus promoting social change (WiA 8: 41–42) reflects the responsibility Kant assigns to individual citizens for addressing injustices accumulated over generations. In my view, Kant's moral philosophy provides key hermeneutical and normative resources to address contemporary expressions of social suffering, as it attempts to strengthen the metaphysical principles of legal and political philosophy in their response to crises such as poverty and marginalization. Put differently, Kant's practical thought reveals the responsibility of those subjects able to grasp

---

to shed light on the suffering and distress ensuing from the insertion of the human being in a social space where he must thrive through his faculties and merits. In this way, it aims to inspect the impact of being surrounded by others, with whom he compares his achievements. Moreover, I also explore social suffering of non-human beings such as animals and the mentally ill, insofar as in my account the boundaries of social life entail an interaction with non-human beings and human beings that do not meet the requirements of technical, pragmatic, and moral autonomy.

the 'general injustice' of massive economic inequality. In this sense, Kant's moral writings do not merely support the idea of a subject insensitive to 'the suffering of others'. On the contrary, they also outline a duty to shape a citizenry aware of local and global interdependence and of the cooperation necessary for all human beings to be able to fulfil their potential. In this vein, in the *Doctrine of Virtue*, Kant urges visiting prisons, hospitals, and slums in order to nurture a more consistent practical judgement, insofar as witnessing this "unliveable life" might allow us to step into the shoes of societies' most vulnerable members. This Element attempts to provide some guidance in navigating Kant's account of social vulnerability, aiming to determine what role Kant envisions for the subject in guaranteeing the maintenance of those marginalized members of society as essential, albeit passive, members of the commonwealth.

First, I inspect how Kant addresses human dignity and the role he assigns to social suffering in his moral theory. Here, I make particular note of Kant's understanding of suffering as an experience able to reveal certain vulnerabilities of the human will, such as the fear of one requiring aid in the future. In this vein, I claim that Kant's reluctance to place a value on the emotional experience of pain and frustration meshes with a moral ideal that aims to diminish social suffering and maximize human flourishing. Second, I address the social experience of suffering as a pedagogical tool able to strengthen the subject's sense of moral obligation, while also considering whether Kant extends his recognition of suffering to animals and the mentally ill. Here, I posit that, even if animals and the mentally ill cannot claim the same rights as humans, they are beneficiaries of the duty not to be abused or mistreated as mere means. In this way, I will stress that non-human beings and those suffering from mental illness represent two cases that help to delimit the boundaries of social interaction and cooperation in the human commonwealth. I point out that humans depend on livestock for the development of society, and that even though the mentally ill may not be able to fulfil any functional contribution to the commonwealth, they still deserve to be treated with dignity as human beings. In this sense, the boundaries of Kant's recognition of suffering are wider than initially supposed. Third, I focus on Kant's analysis of poverty and the moral duty of beneficence – which goes beyond mere benevolence – to determine whether he understands material vulnerability as a potential source of social suffering. In this section, I consider Kant's discussion of outcast individuals, our duties towards others, and the limitations of the beneficence displayed by self-sufficient subjects as crucial for examining this issue. Finally, in the fourth section, I turn to Kant's specific treatment of women's suffering within a patriarchal and oppressive society as a challenge to be addressed. Here, I take into account both correspondence with his young admirer Maria von Herbert, as well as his suggestions to attenuate the legal and social condemnation of women giving birth to children conceived outside of wedlock. Ideally, these four sections will provide a comprehensive overview of Kant's elusive account of social suffering as a multifaceted phenomenon intertwined with the application of moral theory to social interaction. Moreover, I argue that this interpretation of Kant is able to provoke relevant discussion regarding contemporary social issues. While this Element does not shy away from the limitations of applying Kant's approach to social suffering in a contemporary context, it also asserts that Kant's legal and political philosophy fosters a transformation of society that does reckon with the unacceptable abuse and exploitation of human beings and animals.

2 Kant's Approach to Human Dignity: At the Cross-roads of Religion, Morals, and Anthropology

It is beyond doubt that Kant's view regarding the human experience of suffering is severe. In fact, it could be claimed that for Kant, no amount of human pain is truly unbearable, as he considers that a patient and resilient subject will be able to overcome all pain. In his writings on religion, when discussing the amount of grief a human may endure, Kant often describes Jesus Christ as the most perfect example of enduring suffering, and thus as one who personified goodness. In this vein, Christ can be seen as an unsurpassable moral ideal: one who went far beyond the human duty to spread the good insofar as he took 'upon himself all sufferings, up to the most ignominious death, for the good of the world and even for his enemies' (Rel 6: 61). This account implies a challenge for human beings, insofar as their capacity to endure pain is compared with Christ, conflating both divine and human dimensions. At the same time, it shows how human virtue involves a struggle pitting external obstacles and inner temptations against the fulfilment of moral obligation.

This religious rationale of enduring suffering as a moral duty does not lead to the claim that *vulnerability* is a human trait in need of protection, as moral personality does not overlap with human frailty and helplessness. Rather, it urges the subject to control her own desires and interests in order to offer God an image of the humanity in her that is able to please Him. Moreover, the death of Christ as the apogee of suffering displays, in Kant's view, the effective reality of the principle of the good on earth, achieving the 'greatest influence' on the hearts of those living during any historical period, because of 'the contrast between the freedom of the children of heaven and the bondage of a mere son of earth' (Rel 6: 82) that such a death embodies. As a result, the feeling of the insignificance of the individual subject entailed by such a religious ideal is also understandable. Furthermore, it is also comprehensible that Kant emphasizes a moral disposition that he defines as 'humility *(humilitas moralis)*' (DV 6: 435) – the contrary of 'moral arrogance' (*arrogantia moralis*) (DV 6: 435) – as that recommended for abiding with the moral law. In fact, this confirms that Kant's reasoning reflects a chasm between the Christian Son of God's capacity for enduring suffering and the 'son of the earth', who must enlarge his perspective to become a 'citizen of the earth' (Relf 1170, 15: 517).[3] Consequently, the religious approach to suffering does not support seeing its human expression as a moral and social injustice.

Given these issues, the connection Kant makes between the human experience of suffering and the extreme manifestation of it in Christ does not appear to be the most intuitive path for examining the phenomenon of suffering and how the subject should mitigate it in society. That said, the contrast between the human and the godly may help us to better grasp the role of finitude in human moral and social development: in comparison with Christ, the human beings are able to endure much less physical and moral suffering. Kant thus recommends that the moral agent sharpens their conscience to avoid unwittingly or deliberately neglecting atonement for morally wrong actions. For example, to summon a priest or a clergyman to one's deathbed to comfort the dying person for their own 'moral sufferings' rather than their 'physical sufferings' would mean, in Kant's view, 'to administer opium to conscience instead' (Rel 8: 78). Such a conduct is thus regarded as a misdeed insofar as it undermines the moral accountability of the subject, given that 'moral sufferings' likely involve culpable omissions and condemnable actions that one may attempt to disguise.

This religious context of suffering helps us to understand why the human experience of affliction and malaise does not prompt empathy in Kant's writings. A closer approach to Kant's view of human dignity will allow us to further this analysis. First, however, it is useful to note that in Kant's main writings on religion, he blames human cohabitation within society for moral vices such as '[e]nvy, addiction to power, avarice, and the malignant inclinations associated with these' (Rel 6: 93). Kant argues that it is the comparison of one's own possessions and capacities with those of others that makes the subject aware of her social and economic power or lack thereof. For Kant, these and other similar social pathologies are not characteristics of a particularly perverse society, but rather, any collection of human beings living together is enough for these vices to arise: 'it suffices that they are there, that they surround him, and that they are human beings, and they will mutually corrupt each other's moral disposition and make one another evil' (Rel 6: 94). This argument, which Kant deploys as he dissects the sundry dispositions of the human mind, highlights virtue – not sociability – as primary outcome of the fulfilment of moral character.

---

[3] For the difference between these terms see Taraborrelli (2019: 19–20).

In his *Lectures on Anthropology*, Kant also highlights society as a source of suffering and malaise, an appraisal that shares many features with Rousseau's misanthropic assessment of it (Anth-Fried 25: 684–689; Anth-Mron 25: 1419–1420). Differently from Rousseau, however, Kant proposes we acknowledge that societies entail advantages unattainable in the state of nature.[4] In this vein, the depiction of society as a space of 'unsocial sociability' (IUH 8: 24), in which some individuals aim to get 'other human beings' inclinations into [their] power' (Anth § 84, 7: 271)[5], supports the idea that intelligible structures must guide the creation of a commonwealth as an achievement of public justice. Thus, human dignity must be protected in society through a justification different from that of the religious contrast of the human being with God, insofar as the moral horizon of a realm of ends works as an intelligible structure aiming to protect all subjects from unacceptable social injustices. The following subsections will inspect the role of moral tenets in the formation of a peaceful and cohesive commonwealth, whose members should contribute towards eliminate unnecessary social suffering from the earth.

2.1 Kant's Account of Human Dignity

There has been much discussion in recent decades as to whether according to Kant's practical philosophy human dignity is a matter of basic human rights or an outcome of the fulfilment of the moral law. As Oliver Sensen claimed in a groundbreaking essay (Sensen 2011, passim), Kant does not address dignity as a universal, metaphysical dimension of human existence, but as the result of one's conduct meeting the requirements of moral autonomy. In line with this dynamic and relational account of human dignity, it is not surprising that Kant does not show, for instance, any enthusiasm for treatments promising to extend human life, as such a prolonging could also result in a life unable to meet the requirement of moral autonomy, as would be the case of someone only able to perform basic animal functions rather than utilize their higher human faculties (CF 7: 114). The problem here is that when existence is reduced to mere 'animal functions', this gives rise to an utterly insufficient development of the human

---

[4] See this usual rebuke of Kant's reading of Rousseau's account of the antithesis natural order/civil order in Anth-Mron 25: 1420: '[Rousseau] attended only to the harms that the departure from the state of nature seems to have caused, but did not attend to the advantages arising through the culture of the human being; this opposition between the animal and spiritual nature of the human being itself ultimately contributes to the production of the final destiny of the human being.'

[5] Kant's theory of society stresses three social passions or manias — for honour, for dominance, and for possession —, which reduce others to a mere instrumental standing, insofar as they view them as mere 'tools of one's will' (Anth § 84, 7: 271). Such an anthropological landscape sketches a horizon of reification that morality is intended to curb, even if Kant does not deliver a systematic account of this.

mind. In the third part of his writing, *The Conflict of the Faculties,* Kant seems to be influenced by Latin Antiquity's account of the value of life as he discusses psychological traits that further his misgivings about compassion and sympathy as drives allegedly able to ground moral life.

The *Anthropology from a Pragmatic Point of View* (§ 66) observes how the subject tends to minimize the pain of others while exaggerating their own. The following excerpt provides further evidence for Kant's melancholic view of human nature: 'it is not exactly the nicest observation about human beings the fact that their enjoyment increases through the comparison with other's pain, while their own pain is diminished through comparison with similar or even greater sufferings of others' (Anth § 66, 7: 238).[6] At the same time, however, Kant promptly appends this observation to state that this problematic quality of the human mind needn't necessarily hinder the moral character of the subject. This minimizing of the pain of others stems from the *imagination*, a faculty not intended to lead to rational decisions, but rather to relax the mind from higher epistemic functions. Other passages from this writing highlight that attending the theatre teaches the public 'to suffer through the power of imagination' (Anth 7: 239). Yet in the 'theatre' of daily life, imagination appears as a faculty that compares our own pain with the misfortune of others or with worse evils avoided, so that '[t]he misfortune of someone who has broken his leg can be made more bearable if he is shown that he could easily have broken his neck (Anth 7: 239).' In this context, the imagination, which mainly serves to measure the differences of fortune among human beings, must be overseen by thought, which, as has been said, places the value of life on one's moral conduct and the goals achieved by the subject,[7] rather than in the affective realm.

Following the empirical comparison of individual fortune or misfortune, a key element of the correct assessment of the luck and suffering of others is whether – as Kant stresses in the *Groundwork* – 'an impartial rational spectator' would be pleased by the prosperity of a subject not provided with 'a pure and

---

[6] A similar account appears in the following passage from Lucretius poem 'De rerum natura' that Kant quotes in Anth § 66: *Suave, mari magno turbantibus aequora ventis, / E terra magnum alterius spectare laborem; / Non quia vexari quenquam est iucunda voluptas, / Sed quibus ipse malis careas quia cernere suave est.* Lucretius. [Trans.: What joy it is, when out at sea the stormwinds are lashing the waters, to gaze from the shore at the heavy stress some other man is enduring! Not that anyone's afflictions are in themselves a source of delight; but to realize from what troubles you yourself are free is joy indeed. De Rerum Natura 2. 1–4].

[7] See Anth § 66, 7: 238: '[T]his effect is purely psychological (according to the principle of contrast: *opposita iuxta se posita magis elucescunt*) and has no bearing on the moral matter of perhaps wishing suffering on others so that we can feel the comfort of our own condition all the more deeply. One sympathizes with others by means of the power of imagination (for instance, when one sees someone who has lost his balance and is about to fall, one spontaneously and vainly leans toward the opposite side, in order to as it were place him back into balance again), and one is only happy not to be entwined in the same fate'.

good will' (G 4: 393), as it is the basic condition to be worthy of happiness. Other passages from the *Lectures on Ethics* proceed in the opposite direction, as the *Lecture on Ethics Vigilantius* stresses that 'to feel a positive joy at the suffering of another' (Eth-Vigil § 119, 27: 687) makes of the spectator someone ignominious. It must be emphasized that here imagination is seen as unable to develop the moral destiny of the human being, as it primarily considers the external fortune or misfortune that befalls subjects rather than the effort they apply in developing and strengthening their moral character. In other words, the imagination does not consider the moral foundations of a life, sufficing with simply appraising the outward appearance. We must also understand Kant's suggestion to adopt a perspective that promotes continual action and dissuades accumulating enjoyment within this context. In his remarks on the source of the scourge of boredom, Kant posits that idleness reflects a lack of the feeling of living able to seize the subject, as she does not steer her own will, but rather searches for activities to 'fill up time' and thus struggles with the 'abhorrence, ill-humour and disgust' (Eth-Collins 27: 381) that results when wasted time meets human subjectivity. This line of reasoning confirms that Kant's theory of morals requires the subject previously learn to live, as this forms a reliable foundation for moral behaviour, which in turn makes the human being deserving of dignity.

Nonetheless, these observations should not be taken as an indication that Kant views suffering as a phenomenon unfit for philosophical analysis. In this vein, Kant's *Doctrine of Virtue* reminds us that the moral vocation of the human being calls to treat oneself and the others according to the duty of self-esteem, which disavows to 'give himself away for any price' (DV 6: 462). The duty to maintain and protect one's own personality and humanity reveals a marked distance between the *homo phenomenon* and the *homo noumenon*, which depicts not a horizontal relationship, but rather one of subordination. Thus, one should never act as if he is 'master over his personality', or conclude that he might 'dispose over his own substance' (Eth-Vigil 27: 601).

Furthermore, the respect towards a human being seems to depend on her effective capacity to subordinate her will to the moral law. Sensen has highlighted this key nuance of Kant's account of human dignity in sundry papers, stressing that '[w]hat one should respect in others is their freedom. As freedom entails the moral law, one should respect others who are under the moral law and capable of morality.' (Sensen 2011: 133). Put differently, respect as a moral feeling does not result from the attitude that a subordinate – a child or a pupil – has towards his superior, as the former compares his own role with the role of his senior, and morality never results from comparison of civil conditions or social positions. On the contrary, the subject must assume, as a maxim, the limiting of his self-esteem out of respect for the dignity of humanity in others (DV 6: 449).

I follow Sensen in his claim that Kant's conception of dignity differs from contemporary approaches, insofar as he affirms that '[b]y itself dignity does not play a foundational role for Kant' (Sensen 2011: 203), as dignity does not reveal why morality, understood as acting in accordance with respect to the moral law, should take priority over acting following one's own inclinations. As Sensen upholds, Kant's conception of dignity should not be viewed as a disavowal of contemporary accounts of the value of human life, but rather as a path able to lay a foundation for a rational sense of human existence. Perhaps Kant's confession of his indebtedness to Rousseau might shed further light on the distance between our contemporary perspective on human dignity and Kant's arguments.[8] Kant admits that it was Rousseau who showed him which capacities express the sense of humanity, the ultimate value of human beings, and thus urge safeguarding the 'rights of humanity' (OFBS 20: 44). Even if Kant affirms, in the *Groundwork*, that 'dignity [has] an unconditional, incomparable worth' (G 4: 436), Sensen (2011: 160–165) reminds us that Kant never grounds morality on this inner worth, but rather on our use of our own freedom (Refl 18: 181).

Other writings, and particularly Kant's lectures on natural right, show Kant's claims that the condition of a human being as an end in itself presupposes that he has no equivalent. Equivalency can only be seen in the case of things with external value. Thus, the value assigned to persons impedes their oppression or domination as if they were mere means, for '[t]his limitation is based on the condition of universal consent with the will of others as far as possible. There is nothing except a human being that can be posited as more worthy of respect than the right of human beings' (L-NR 27: 1319). Passages such as this highlight the obligation of every human being to engage in a dialogue with the will of others in serving the ideal of humanity they are intended to achieve. Again, this is not the case of things, as they are used according to their price and the external value they assume based on supply and demand.

A similar rationale determines that human beings are unable to dispose of their own lives, as the body is neither a contingent feature of human life nor merely one state of life among others, but rather its organic and material condition. Kant draws a powerful image illustrating this in the *Lecture on*

---

[8] See OFBS 20: 44: 'There was a time when I believed this constituted the honor of humanity, and I despised the people, who know nothing. Rousseau set me right about this. This binding prejudice disappeared. I learned to honor humanity, and I would find myself more useless than the common laborer if I did not believe this attitude of mine can give worth to all others in establishing the rights of humanity.'

Ethics Collins, when he writes that 'if we could slip out of one body and enter another, like a country, then we could dispose over the body' (Eth-Collins 27: 369). On the contrary, however, the human body is the material condition indispensable for exercising freedom, which consequently cannot seek to destroy or abolish it. Kant stresses later in this passage that freedom is embodied in us through the body, which thus 'constitutes a part of the self' (Eth-Collins 27: 369).[9] In this sense, to use one's will to take one's own life would imply a self-destructive action worthy of condemnation. Another *Lecture on Ethics* – focusing on the metaphysics of morals: *Vigilantius* – underlines the strict duty to preserve one's own life, stemming from the respect for one's own personhood as a rational being. Hence, even the most unbearable suffering and pain could not legitimate committing suicide, as classical morals argued (Eth-Vigil § 92, 27: 628). Even if Kant was deeply influenced by classical Stoicism, he has plain misgivings about the ideal of existence ensuing from it – as shown Kant argues that even the cruellest suffering could be compatible with a worthy life. Yet he also admits that, despite the value of moral ideals, the human being needs certain external, physical conditions to be met so as not to falter in his moral development.

Thus, Kant's account of human dignity gives rise to a duty to take care of one's body, nurturing 'its vigour, activity, strength and courage' (Eth-Collins 27: 380), controlling its impulses, and satisfying its basic needs. Yet, such a duty to provide the body with all it might require does not address the emotional health and wellness of the subject. Put differently, Kant's theory of virtue seems to urge that the body is maintained in good health as the material side of the will, without further attention to the emotional needs of the human being. Moreover, the subject is invited to take care of his bodily dimension as a human animal, without neglecting his dignity as a rational human being. Consequently, the body appears as a structural feature underpinning any use of freedom, which must be conserved in order to guarantee the moral life of the subject.

As is well known, the principle guiding Kant's treatment of human dignity draws on the imperative of treating others not only as means, but at the same time as ends in themselves according to the self-respect that drives the subject to meet the requirements of his moral destiny (DV § 11, 6: 435). As another passage from the *Doctrine of Virtue* affirms: '[i]t is just in this [to be used not

---

[9] Kant's remarks about the body as a condition for the use of freedom are very close to Hegel's approach to it. See Hegel, GPhR § 48: 60: 'It is only because I in my living body am a free being, that my body cannot be used as a beast of burden. ... It is an irrational and sophistic doctrine, which separates body and soul, calling the soul the thing in itself and maintaining that it is not touched or hurt when the body is wrongly treated, or when the existence of a person is subject to the power of another. ... I exist for others in my body; that I am free for others s the same thing as that I am free in this outward life. If my body is treated roughly by others, I am treated roughly.'

merely as a means, but also as an end] that his dignity (personality) consists, by which he raises himself above all other beings in the world that are not human beings and yet can be used, and so over all *things*' (DV § 38, 6: 462). In contrast with this, behaviours such as seeking to curry the favour of another through hypocrisy and flattery entail a degradation of one's personality, and should be prevented so as to foster the development of morality. As Kant advises, '[our] insignificance as a human animal may not infringe upon [our] consciousness of his dignity as a rational human being' (DV § 11, 6: 435), indicating the means and attitudes that the subject is recommended to adopt to preserve his status as an 'intelligible being'. Put differently, to boast of one's own moral worth by comparing oneself to others is seen as a deplorable conduct. Such behaviours demonstrate both the polarity, and as well as the propinquity, of humility and ambition. These traits, common in any social space, hinder the development of a culture of a social interaction by undermining its commitment to the preservation of human dignity as a common goal.

As the arguments above seek to show, Kant mistrusts in the emotions as a way to analyse the suffering affecting the subject and others. Far from an emotional approach to social suffering, Kant prefers to distinguish between the empirical value of human existence and the moral status all human beings are intended to achieve. Even if all human beings dread becoming subjects of suffering, and feel comparatively lucky upon realizing that others are suffering more than them, the development of moral life must overcome such a standpoint to adopt a moral commitment towards one's own autonomy. Furthermore, moral development involves, in Kant's view, a transformation of the subject's attitude towards his own physical suffering, leading to increased resilience in difficult situations. Even if the human being cannot aspire to moral sainthood, he must improve his perception of affliction and discomfort so as to be able to tolerate them. Naturally, Kant is aware of the role of external aids such as the emotion of hope, and their importance for the human not to falter in the fulfilment of their moral duties. Nevertheless, the emotional spectacle of the suffering of others shows a limited role in determining practical subjectivity in Kant's theory of morals. That said, this does not dispense with the task of examining the function of human pain within the moral pedagogy of his theories.

2.2 The Moral Economy of Kant's Social Emotions: Gender and Class Biases

This subsection addresses Kant's proposal to control the emotions when interacting with others. Kant holds that to make compassion and solidarity the primary reaction to the suffering of others is to contribute to overindulgence and immoderation, attitudes that compromise our morality. Moreover, I seek to show how Kant tends to describe women's perspectives as immature or impractical when reacting to misfortune or injustice affecting other people, as he considers that women are less prepared to develop the disposition to personality due to their 'biological tasks' and natural civil passive character. Furthermore, I will also spotlight some biases in moral perception Kant sees as inherent to privileged social classes, which, in Kant's view hinder the adoption of an impartial and objective standpoint in the face of one's own misfortune. In this way, I aim to shed light on the influence of gender and class on common moral judgements.

While Kant's foundations of morals furnish a universal account of moral autonomy and duty, it is also evident that he addresses human emotions differently along gender lines. In this vein, analysing what Kant views as the appropriate emotional reaction to the suffering and distress of others may prove valuable. For example, weeping in solidarity with the mourning of others (which he openly disclaims as 'disgusting music' (Anth § 76, 7: 255–256)) is rebuked by Kant as 'feminine' or 'effeminate' in men. By contrast, the masculine character should limit itself to displaying a 'powerless sympathy with others' suffering' (Anth § 76, 7: 255–256). While this might manifest as being 'moved to tears' (Anth § 76, 7: 255–256), it is not considered behaving in a shameful manner. Kant is not suggesting that his audience and readers react insensitively towards the hardship of a friend, an acquaintance or even a stranger, but rather avoid crying even when the subject cannot help but moved by the story he is hearing. Despite this gendered view, this does not necessarily mean that women are seen as reprehensible, as Kant also asserts that they have been educated to assume every misfortune with the utmost patience, able 'to make suffering (enduring) imperceptible through habit' (Anth § 77, 7: 257). Indeed, to a certain extent, Kant even favours cultivating 'feminine' emotional traits, such as a duty to maintain 'a constantly cheerful heart'.[10] Remarks like this one highlight the central role of inner joy in the development of moral character: 'undeserved sufferings' such as betrayal, ingratitude, or love spurned have the potential to make the subject lose any desire for social interaction, while a light-hearted point of view fosters social participation.

Kant also references the case of virtuous individuals who descend into misanthropy as a result of their focus on virtue: 'here are those who from an exaggerated principle of virtue remove themselves from social life, because their days are embittered by many undeserved sufferings' (Eth-Vigil § 115,

---

[10] While Kant often relates these traits to Epicurus' *voluptas*, they should not be confused with *voluptuousness* (Eth-Vigil §104, 27: 646).

27: 672). Such a pathological cultivation of moral virtue would not coincide with the case of the 'negative misanthrope' (*anthropophobus*), who does not display a tendency towards social coexistence. In contrast with misanthropy stemming from a pathological cultivation of moral virtue, 'the negative misanthrope *anthropophobus*, i.e., one who withdraws himself from everyone, because he is unable to love them' is completely devoid of love for others and thus considers that 'everyone is oblivious to all the respect due to himself' (Eth-Vigil § 115, 27: 672). Consequently, in this account of the emotions fostering universal love for all human beings and peaceful social interaction (whose normative status is not clarified by Kant) passions such as *revenge* are not seen as legitimate, as these involve 'an immediate pleasure at the suffering of the offender' (Eth-Vigil § 119, 27: 689), and thus reveal a hatred for humanity. Another passage from the *Lecture on Ethics Vigilantius* illustrates the emotional discipline required by morality, discussing feelings and affects traditionally assigned to women:

> [N]either the greatest advantages, nor the highest degree of wellbeing, nor the most excruciating pains and even irremediable bodily sufferings can give a man the authority to take his own life, to escape from anguish and enter earlier upon a hoped-for higher happiness. The preservation of his life is a strict duty, resting upon respect for the personhood accorded to him as a rational being, and of which, as a sensuous being, he may not divest himself (Eth-Vigil § 92, 27: 628).

Such an account hints at Kant's stoic influence, which he mostly views as a male behaviour, while also highlighting the vulnerability of human nature in its struggle against the powerful threats to morality inherent in society. However, it is also indisputable that in Kant's view, 'even personal slavery, or the harshest bodily suffering, can be compatible with a man's freedom' (Eth-Vigil § 92, 27: 628). Kant's moral theory urges engaging in a thoughtful exchange with fellow members of society, and he accurately analyses the ideas of 'taking something to heart' and 'bearing something consciously in mind'. In Kant's view, the latter degrades our humanity insofar as it leaves us bereft of self-esteem, which every human being deserves as a result of their personhood. Moreover, Kant focuses on human beings, who, unlike animals, are able to develop an intellectual experience of distress and pain by translating sensory impressions and perceptions into mental representations, and redefining those sensations in terms of fortune and misfortune (Anth-Fried 25: 567–568). It is noteworthy that class biases are also mentioned in Kant's account of unrecommended practical reactions to personal setbacks, as being accustomed to economic prosperity prevents a full-fledged development of one's own moral character. Furthermore, Kant associates the evaluation of luck or the lack thereof to one's contingent lifespan, in which some become accustomed to wealth and luxury while others consistently face adversity. The well off, for instance, appear less capable of impartially assessing setbacks they may encounter, insofar as they are not accustomed to taking into account the misfortune of others, or to examining their own relative fortune across the arc of their lives. Here, it seems privileged subjects are "making a mountain out of a molehill", as their elitist socialization undermines not only their insertion into society, but also their subjection to the rules of interdependence and legal equality.

Kant's mature moral theory confirms his reluctance to make compassion for suffering an appropriate source of moral motivation. According to the universal duty to love all human beings and to respect the universal justice that must rule society, all subjects must strive to improve the living conditions of other members of their own community. The imagination, however, continues to be blamed as a faculty allowing the subject to 'be infected by ... pain' (DV § 34 6: 457), increasing the number of those suffering, even if only by one person. As Kant adds later in this passage, 'there cannot possibly be a duty to increase the ills in the world and so to do good *from compassion*' (DV § 34 6: 457). Such a behaviour, in Kant's view, would also degrade human dignity, as it stems from the pity the subject feels towards others, without considering the worthiness for happiness the sufferer might display.

The role of sheer determination in responding adequately to misfortune is mostly tackled in Anthropology writings, which focus on the construction of a sound reflective subjectivity. In this vein, in the *Lecture of Anthropology Friedländer,* Kant further examines the distance between a sensory and a rational satisfaction resulting from the spectacle of the fortune or misfortune of others (Anth-Fried 25: 610). While rational satisfaction arises from rational sympathy, the judgement of the senses merely triggers a sensory satisfaction.[11] Moreover, in judging our private lives, we lack the ability to observe our circumstances with the distance necessary for rational evaluation. Finally, while rational sympathy interprets the distress, pain, or misfortune of others as evils that must be removed from the world through practical effort, the

---

[11] Vilhauer (2024: 4–9) has accurately traced the Kant's different approach to 'rational' and 'natural sympathy' in five of his lectures on anthropology and morals ranging over twenty years, which offers a quite large outlook over the reasons legitimating such a conceptual distinction. On the role that productive imagination yields in Kant's double-sided account of sympathy see Vilhauer (2024: 57) 'In natural sympathy, I find myself passively driven into this imaginary standpoint by my inclinations, and I passively furnish it with sensible content via inclination-driven associations with the concepts the other shares. In rational sympathy, I actively place myself in it, and carefully associate the sensible content that I think will help me sympathize correctly.'

impassioned pleas of those seeking to stir our conscience to action will dampen our trust in their testimony, until we ultimately lose the willingness to provide help. In Kant's view, these disparate reactions demonstrate the emotions and passions as unreliable guides for the moral development of the subject, justifying the unwavering attitude that the moral subject should show towards them:

> However, we do not sympathize with others' agitations of the mind, even if we sympathize with their fate. For example, we sympathize with another's sadness and pain, but if he begins to lament and bursts out weeping, then we distance ourselves from him. We do not sympathize with another's passions and violent agitations of mind. What is more, our sympathy is then diminished (Anth-Fried 25: 610).

In this excerpt, Kant aims to describe a key psychological trait of the human mind, associating intense displays of emotion (wailing, sobbing) with the narration of personal tragedy. The contribution to the happiness of others as ends does not contradict with the wider moral duty that the subject must pursue according to Kant's view of human societal coexistence. Certain temperaments, (particularly the sanguine – which I will address later –), are overly sensitive to the suffering of others. Individuals with these temperaments are soft-hearted and easily affected by others' pain and lamentations, which impairs them from impartially judging controversial issues, as they are unacquainted with the conditions of justice, (OFBS 2: 222) and threatens transforming them into 'a tender-hearted idler' (OFBS 2: 216). As seen in this section, Kant prioritizes action over passivity in the formation of moral personality, a distinction that can be also explored through the aforementioned difference between 'taking the suffering of friends to heart' and 'bearing them in mind'. While the former implies consciousness of the pain suffered by others, the latter makes the subject herself feel unhappy, as she assumes the pain of others as a personal affliction. The upshot of this analysis is that 'no external ill can make us so unhappy, that we no longer merit being alive, as solely the actions contrary to morality [can do]' (Anth-Fried 25: 597). In this way, Kant's approach to the pain and suffering of others consistently views these phenomena through the lens of moral perfection, a universal aim which human beings should strive for and one that reciprocally favours the satisfaction of their material needs.

In a nutshell, Kant claims that often, the moral attitude that the subject shows towards the suffering of others depends on sensitive, emotional drives resulting from gender and/or social class, characteristics clouding moral perception, which stems from the respect for the moral law, rather than from feelings or emotions of sympathy and pity. In this context, it is important to keep in mind that in Kant's view, the true value of life could never be derived from passive feelings and sensations, but rather from the actions the subject undertakes by decisions following moral – and not natural or mechanical – maxims (CJ § 83 5: 434f.).

2.3 Cultivating the Art of Sympathy: Taming Egoism and Averting Misanthropy

Kant's moral philosophy accurately analyses the responses to the suffering of others that meet the condition of respect for the humanity embodied in all human beings. Nevertheless, it is significant that the pedagogical examples of sound moral character that Kant makes use of in his moral writings are expected to leave a deep impact on the human mind, at times more vivid than the grief ensuing from blatant injustice and institutional disrepair. Notably, the development of morality involves a dimension of assumed suffering, insofar as moral progress often demands renouncing the allure of satisfying human inclinations. Put slightly differently, to embrace moral maxims for guiding our actions requires foregoing much happiness arising from social interaction, as the ultimate meaning of human action must be viewed from a moral standpoint. In this vein, it is helpful to remember that the path to virtue is paved with great effort, which nothing demonstrates better, in Kant's view, than the impressive resistance and suffering of an honest individual. What's more, this should inspire the highest respect in adolescents, that is, those still unversed in the practical field (KPrR 5: 156). How though, to convey to a teenager that pure morality is a touchstone from which to judge the value of every action? Furthermore, would sacrificing one's most enjoyable emotions so as to abide by moral principles be experienced as grief, as seen in the aforementioned example of Christ? The following excerpt from the *Critique of Practical Reason,* in which an individual refuses to join calumniators intending to slander an innocent and powerless person, displays the powerful effect that an honest individual's resistance to evil should exert over young people:

> then my young listener will be raised step by step from mere approval to admiration, from that to amazement, and finally to the greatest veneration and a lively wish that he himself could be such a man (though certainly not in such circumstances); and yet virtue is here worth so much only because it costs so much, not because it brings any profit (KPrR 5: 156).

This exhortation stresses that the subject must be prepared to assume the high costs that morality exacts on seeking one's own happiness or the expectation of any empirical profit ensuing from such action. Moreover, it encourages displaying morality as untainted by empirical elements as possible, through examples of holiness and virtue that exhibit the suffering that must be accepted to attain those exalted levels of moral perfection. The passage also stresses that the young listener will seek to behave like such an exemplary man, albeit 'certainly not in such circumstances'. Such an account legitimates the role that suffering might fulfil in the moral self-transformation of the subject, whose inferior appetitive faculty dissuades him from accepting any eventual pain and from renouncing the pleasures of life. In his portrayal of an honest man resisting the pressure to partake in the arraignment of an innocent person, Kant 'represents him at the moment he wishes that he had never lived to see the day that exposed him to such unutterable pain and yet remains firm in his resolution to be truthful' (KPrR 5: 156). The excerpt adds that the adolescent listening to this story would pass from mere approval to admiration, until ultimately feeling amazement and being seized by 'the greatest veneration' (KPrR 5: 156). Kant closes this pedagogical digression by stating that to exhibit virtue untainted by any consideration to personal well-being and comfort has a deeper influence on the human heart than virtue diluted with these secondary considerations. Moreover, the reasoning ensuing from the higher faculty of desire should not overshadow or annul the effects that the lower faculty of desire brings about in the human mind. As shown by this example, the witnessing of the suffering of others fulfils a key role in fostering moral dispositions aimed at making the human commonwealth a network of effective interdependence and mutual support.

Even if the sacrifice of one's own comfort is necessary for the moral development of the subject, Kant had acknowledged, since the pre-critical period, the helpful effect of 'a kindly participation in the fate of other people' (OFBS 2: 215) to forestall or remove undesirable harms from the social realm. Such a moral disposition towards the misfortune and pain of others leads to developing means that prevent the subject from slipping into melancholy and rendering him unable to positively contribute to the happiness of his commonwealth. Yet the 'natural' human reaction towards the suffering of a beloved or an acquaintance does not provide an objective measurement of the proper response to the suffering of others. Hence, determining the proper feedback to hardships suffered by others requires previously understanding the shortcomings of a prompt, supportive emotional response. In this vein, it is noteworthy that Kant traces an inconsistency in the emotional dynamics of sympathy, as this may lead to a melancholic compassion focusing on the misfortune of an individual person, while simultaneously neglecting evils that may affect a larger number of people. In this context, Kant's uses eloquent examples from warfare to highlight the asymmetry evident when human judgement more easily empathizes with an individual misfortune than collective destruction:

> A suffering child, an unhappy though upright woman may fill our heart with this melancholy, while at the same time we may coldly receive the news of

a great battle in which, as may readily be realized, a considerable part of humankind must innocently suffer dreadful evils. Many a prince who has averted his countenance from melancholy for a single unfortunate person has at the same time given the order for war, often from a vain motive. There is here no proportion in the effect at all, so how can one say that the general love of humankind is the cause? (OFBS 2: 216f.).

The excerpt effectively demonstrates how the pitfalls of human perception hinder the moral agent's correct valuation and decision-making when regarding different scales of suffering. This partiality of sympathy also explains the *Doctrine of Virtue*'s strong misgivings about the benefits of compassion, which functions as a sensitive impulse to share in the sufferings and joys of others. At the same time, however, this writing also highlights the 'duty to sympathize actively in [the] fate of others' (DV § 35, 6: 457), which entails cultivating natural feelings of solidarity (a disposition underpinning sympathy) based in moral principles. Thus, Kant opposes avoiding 'the places where the poor who lack the most basic necessities are to be found but rather [recommends] to seek them out, and not to shun sickrooms or debtors' prisons' (DV § 35, 6: 457), as he argues that the contemplation of such places of suffering can foster aesthetical support useful in fulfilling moral duty.

Before interpreting this remark, it will be helpful to break down the meaning of two German terms, *Mitgefühl* and *Mitleidenschaft*, both similar to the English *compassion*, but containing a key nuance that stresses the agency and passivity, respectively, contained in them.[12] The first term 'shared feeling' – *Mitgefühl* – plays a key role in Kant's moral theory, as it generally helps the agent to put himself in the place of another person, a moral operation that Scottish and French authors such as Adam Smith and Sophie de Grouchy had previously discussed as a phenomenon related to sympathy. This feeling clearly differs, in Kant's view, from 'compassion' (*Mitleidenschaft; Mitleid*), defined as *humanitas aesthetica*, that is, a mere receptivity to the feeling of joy and sadness of others, opposed to reflexive sympathy, and more akin to the receptivity to warmth or the contagion of illnesses. Hence, in contrast with sympathy through sensitive contagion, the *Mitgefühl* rather helps to fulfil the moral law, insofar as it reveals the human being's capacity to share the feelings of others, according to the *humanitas practica* (DV 6: 456–457), going beyond mere sensitivity to feel morally co-responsible for their fate. Already in the pre-critical period, Kant assessed human temperaments as a significant natural foundation for a subsequent moral character. In this context, Kant asserts that the sanguine temperament would be incapable of attaining a true moral sympathy – given

---

[12] See the account of both terms in Wehofsits (2016: 132–160).

their soft-hearted nature, the sanguine person immediately shares the joyfulness and suffering of others, just as he also receives the other various impressions around him. Thus, Kant discards him the sanguine individual as a mere friend, one who easily changes with the social environment:

> Today he will entertain you with his friendliness and good sorts, tomorrow, when you are ill or misfortunate, he will feel genuine and unfeigned compassion, but he will quietly slip away until the circumstances have changed. He must never be a judge (OFBS 2: 222).

The passage clearly discards this psychological profile as a reliable observer of the suffering of others. Other passages from the *Observations about the Feeling of Beauty and Sublime* also hint to the key difference between aesthetic and practical sympathy: the former appears too weak and temporary to prompt 'a kindly participation in the fate of other people, to which principles of virtue likewise lead'. (OFBS 2: 215–216). Moreover, the empathy with the feeling of others is fleeting, and does not foster any connection with universal principals, which must guide the maxims of a subject in order for them to behave coherently with a moral conduct consistent with Kant's total framework of human action. Under further consideration, one finds that however endearing the quality of sympathy may be, it does not contain within it the dignity of virtue. Furthermore, as Timmermann (2016: 731–732) has highlighted, the recommendation to visit hospitals, asylums, and other marginalized places does not apply to everyone. In fact, Kant includes an observation in his published Anthropology closely intertwined with the analysis of compassion in § 35 of the *Doctrine of Virtue*. In § 32 of *Anthropology from a Pragmatic Point of View*, focusing on the power of imagination, he references a report by the physician of Kassel Christian Friedrich Michaelis[13] containing the anecdote of a soldier in North America who 'fell into a violent frenzy', stoking similar reactions in some bystanders of the incident. Thus, in the case of hypochondriac persons, Kant decidedly counsels against visiting 'lunatic asylums out of curiosity' (Anth § 32, 7: 179), as he considers weak-nerved people unable to impartially judge these experiences, and likely to become victims of mental disorder themselves.

Despite his awareness of the selfishness ingrained in the human condition, Kant affirms that the human being is destined to develop a moral approach to the suffering of others, resulting from the natural drive to sympathize with the distress and anguish we perceive in others. This moral recommendation to become acquainted with the miserable goes beyond the 'natural instinct in

---

[13] See Michaelis (1785: 114–117). About the 'contagion' as a practical phenomenon see Hatfield, Cacioppo, and Rapson (1993).

man to be jealous' (Eth-Vigil § 121, 27: 698), which, for instance, hinders a healthy person from grasping the sufferings of an ill person (Eth-Vigil § 121, 27: 694). In this vein, Kant quotes La Rochefoucauld, insofar as the French anthropologist avows that 'in the sufferings of our best friends there is something that does not wholly displease us' (Eth-Vigil § 121, 27: 697). This also explains why Kant would choose not to ground his moral theory on sensitivity or sympathy but rather in the subjection of the human faculty of desire to the moral law. Kant also stresses the fact that those experiencing suffering such as illness might feel some envy towards those not affected by this misfortune, even wishing that they may also 'be plunged into [such a situation]' (Eth-Vigil § 121, 27: 694). Thus, Kant's psychological analysis posits that every human being desires, to some extent, that even his closest friends do not achieve a state of complete happiness, for this would lead to unbearable jealousy. At the same time, when friends are beset by unfortunate circumstances, the subject has the chance to feel superior to them. This selfish, emotional basis of the human mind, however, must be distinguished from the attitude of a misanthrope, who feels hatred for other human beings, and who Kant views as regrettable elements of social life, insofar as they display a complete lack of respect for humanity and its moral value[14]:

> since everyone must wish for the well-being of others, the man who hates seems clearly to be in conflict with his own principles; he sees himself in a state where he can censure himself, and must even reject himself; he feels himself to be acting contrary to the end of humanity in his own person, if he is able to feel a positive joy at the sufferings of another, and still more so if he has himself caused this evil in the first place. *He is an object worthy of hatred*, just as the injured party, who is unable to bear his sufferings, can still remain a lovable one (Eth-Vigil § 119, 27: 687).

This extreme case of misanthropy discloses a clear incapacity to empathize with others, and such individuals renounce protecting and contributing to the thriving of humanity in themselves and other human beings. However, this anthropological pathology must be accurately distinguished from the societal obstacles the subject encounters that inhibit him from impartially grasping the joys and sufferings of his fellow humans. As Kant affirms in his main writing on religion, any time subjects belong to a social space, they are likely to compare themselves and their social status to that of others, substituting self-love, the foundation of a 'predisposition to humanity' with 'the inclination *to gain worth in the opinion of others*' (Rel 6: 27). While initially, the subject seeks merely not to be despised

---

[14] See Kant's definition of callousness (*animus frigidus*) and *solipsismus* with regard to philanthropy in Eth-Vigil § 115, 27: 672.

when compared to others, he progressively fears that other members of society display more abilities and possessions than he, bringing about a state of constant anxiety. These 'vices of *culture*' (Rel 6: 27) result in maleficent emotional attitudes such as *envy, ingratitude,* and *joy in others' misfortunes*, which should be decidedly criticized by a social theory aware of both the pitfalls of civil society and its possibilities enabled by the duties of the subject.[15]

3 Enlarging the Framework of Suffering: How to Treat Animals and the Mentally Ill Well?

Kant's practical philosophy extols the respect that should be granted to every human being regarded as a person (DV § 11, 6:434–435), a message also conveyed by the second formulation of the categorical imperative. As is well known, this formula commands understanding the humanity both in us and in others 'always at the same time as an end, never merely as a means'. (G 4:429). This subordination of means to ends provokes key political and civil consequences. For example, this imperative might inspire political agendas requiring that immigrants and foreigners contribute in a perceptible way to the welfare of the host commonwealth. Put differently, to be used as a functional means in society can be proof of the recognition of the moral value of a person, since to be excluded of any meaningful role in a commonwealth would threaten both social and moral membership.[16] The 'virtues of social intercourse' (DV § 48, 6: 473–474) –affability, sociability, hospitality, courtesy, and gentleness – are also quite indicative of the human duty to engage into a system of interdependence with others, complementing the role of labour in achieving this goal (Vrousalis 2022). Even if they remain 'by-products (*parerga*)' of the real virtue, they acquaint subjects with promoting and enlarging social membership.[17] Human beings, however, not only draw on other humans to fulfil their instrumental aims, as shown by their dependence on the animal 'workforce'. Furthermore, the inalienable humanity found in all human beings demands a proper

---

[15] See González (2020: 98): '[C]ulture is a middle ground between nature and morality. It is not simply the result of interactions between natural causes and pragmatic reason, nor it is simply the result of man's moral commitment to taking history by the reins. Rather, it represents reason's ultimate interest in finding a meaning for human experience'.

[16] See a Kant-inspired defence of migration integration as a global social challenge in Mieth and Williams (2022: 221): 'Lack of legal protection, dependency and marginalization fulfil the prophecies of populist rhetoric, that migration diverts resources and fosters criminality. Prohibitions on work may seem to undercut fears that migrants are unwelcome competitors for scarce employment. But their rhetorical effect is to reinforce such fears. Their practical effect is to foster a desperately insecure underclass – people who need not be paid even the legal minimum, who lack any effective rights to safe and decent working conditions, and who can easily be drawn into dangerous or even criminal enterprise.'

[17] I am grateful to Sylvie Loriaux for having alerted me to the transformative social dimension of moral virtues in Kant's view.

commonwealth to care for its mentally ill members on humanitarian grounds, even if they represent a social burden because of their inability to engage in any pragmatic social interaction with others. This section will inspect these cases as issues able to shed light on Kant's account of social suffering.

Kant does not confine the acknowledgement of suffering to humans as unique beings meeting the requirements of a moral subject. Rather, he enlarges the scope of humanity, considering the assistance provided by animals, as well as the mentally ill, insofar as their inability to act as moral agents does not negate their humanity. Both cases motivate diverse arguments and reasonings. While animals may not claim any identification with the moral standing of humans, they may expect that their owners will not mistreat, abuse or torture them, given that they free their owners from performing difficult and tedious tasks and allow them to increase their productivity. The mentally ill, for their part, demonstrate a failure of the faculties of the mind begetting manifold forms of mental illness.[18] Even if Kant advocates for the creation of specific social spaces, such as asylums, to host patients affected by these diseases, he also shows a clear consciousness of the therapeutic role of social interaction in attenuating, to some extent, these afflictions. It must be said that Kant's writing on mental illnesses may seem quite harsh to the contemporary reader, demonstrating little pity for these individuals, who often appear as a completely useless segment of the commonwealth. Moreover, the contemporary interpreter may see the philosopher's suggestion of curing mental illness through social interaction as naive.

It would be also an overstatement to claim that Kant argues for identical claims to justice with regard to animals and the mentally ill. Animals, as non-human living beings that rid humans of burdensome tasks, deserve a sort of *reward* or bounty.[19] Conversely, the mentally ill show themselves incapable of any epistemic and practical autonomy, shifting the responsibility for their care to public and private institutions. Nevertheless, Kant's account of morals and virtue goes beyond the moral status of the human being to shed light on the

---

[18] According to Kant, distinguishing mental illnesses from apparent deficiencies of the mind is crucial. He references a telling anecdote of unsound pedagogical systems, such as the one suffered by the celebrated Jesuit Clavius, whose masters discarded for not being able to compose verses, but who showed outstanding capacities as he began to learn mathematics (MH 2: 260). Thus, Kant considers that detecting the capacities of the student represents a key task of teachers. Moreover, if teachers succeed in recognizing the potential of their students, many alleged mental deficiencies might be averted.

[19] It deserves to be noticed that Kant understands animals as auxiliary species providing helpful services to the human commonwealth, which foster ties of trust and gratitude with human beings. Nevertheless, Kant's reflections on potential rational beings living on other planets disclaim any possibility of a social fruitful interaction with human beings living on earth due to the anthropological divergence between both rational expressions. For instance, the first ones are outlined as beings thinking aloud and incapable of having thoughts they do not utter immediately, which would easily jeopardize any peaceful social life on earth. See Anth 7: 732.

needs of beings which will never attain full-fledged human standing. Put differently, the moral perfection of the subject requires thoughtful treatment, not only of his equals, but also of other animals forming part of his household, as well as other humans unable to accomplish epistemic and moral development. In this regard, while the useful animal must be viewed as a helpful cooperator, the human being suffering from mental disorder deserves to be attended to according to his medical needs. Both cases illustrate Kant's attention to modalities of existence unable to achieve the moral destination of the human being, albeit for different reasons. These beings either maintain close ties with the development of human culture (in the case of animals) or cannot forfeit the respect owed to the humanity in them (in the case of the mentally ill).

3.1 Kant on Animal Suffering

In this subsection, I will aim to grasp some conclusions from Kant's view of animals able to elaborate on his more general theory of human dignity and of personal perfection as a moral task. In fact, Kant's practical philosophy addresses the duties that rational human beings must fulfil '[w]ith regard to the animate but nonrational part of the creation' (DV § 17, 6: 443), even though the latter do not meet all the requirements needed to be considered rational beings. In particular, the §§ 16 and 17 of the *Doctrine of Virtue,* and certain *Lectures on Ethics* – such as *Collins* and *Vigilantius* – contain key remarks on this subject. The *Doctrine of Virtue* rejects the idea that human beings have any direct duties towards animals, as they do not possess any moral standing. Nevertheless, this account admits that animals perform a helpful service to workers, families, and individuals, which adds important nuance to the recognition they deserve from rational human beings.[20] The attachment that humans ought to consecrate to animals takes after the dynamics of social sympathy, as an 'indirect duty' (DV § 34, 6: 456–457) which 'does not constitute moral dispositions' (Eth-Mron 29: 626) – in Kant's account, animals seem to engage into an emotional dialogue with their owners and other humans, even if they do not belong to this species. Kant's view of the ethical treatment of animals has sparked much discussion in recent decades[21], as

---

[20] Such an evaluation of animal cooperation focuses on the fact that the human being understands the utility that he receives from the animal workforce. Even if Kant does not address whether mere comfort and company could be helpful outcomes of human coexistence with domestic animals, I consider that his account would not disavow such perceptions. I am grateful to Sylvie Loriaux for having suggested this to me.

[21] The recent interpretation of Kant's practical philosophy has largely addressed the role of animals in the teleological landscape of rational and non-rational beings on earth. Even if critiques of Kant's view of animals as recipients of indirect duties of virtue have been profuse in the field of applied ethics (Pybus and Broadie 1978; Müller 2022), it is possible to delimit a group of interpreters more friendly towards some promising features of Kant's account (Denis 2000; Timmermann 2005; Kain 2010; Wilson 2012; Korsgaard 2018; Varden 2020b; Salgueiro 2024).

it adopts a recognizable utilitarian standpoint regarding the ties between human beings and animals that has been largely reproved. In discussing some remarks on the value of animals with regard to human actions, some scholars have considered the ecological bonds linking humans and animals in the context of a natural world that must be preserved, protected, and bequeathed to future generations (Svoboda 2015; Vereb 2021).

Kant's account, however, does not make animal beings proper members of society, as their actions merely depend on instinct and thus they are unable to ground moral character on the basis of a disposition to personality. As Kant writes in the *Lecture on Anthropology Menschenkunde* (Anth-Mensch 25: 1033): 'If an animal would know to say 'I', he would be my fellow'. So far, this is not the case of animals, whose analysis has often entailed salient mistakes in Kant's view, as would be the case of scholars as Georg Friedrich Meier, author of *Versuch eines neuen Lehrgebäudes von den Seelen der Thiere* (1749), and Hermann Samuel Reimarus, author of *Allgemeine Betrachtungen über die Triebe der Thiere* (1762). While Kant rebukes physical and philosophical enquiries that blur the boundaries between the animal and the human mind (FS 2: 59), he does not relinquish his view of animal wellness as a societal commitment appropriate to human morality. In Kant's time, the most common argument for viewing animals as fellow beings pointed to their ability to distinguish objects, persons, and qualities as humans do. Yet in Kant's view, such a perceptive capacity does not entail an ability to represent these qualities and understand them as characteristics of things. Discussing the mind of an ox in a pre-critical writing on logic, Kant highlights the difference between the animal and human approximation to reality:

> The door is something which does, it is true, belong to the stall and can serve as a characteristic mark of it. But only the being who forms the judgement: *this door belongs to this stable* has a distinct concept of the building, and that is certainly beyond the powers of animals (FS 2: 59).

Kant adds later in this same text that animals are able '*to differentiate* things from each other' (FS 2: 59), which nevertheless does not imply a clear recognition of the difference between these two objects. In fact, as seen in the previous excerpt, it is only the power of judgement that endows beings with the capacity for consciousness of the logical difference of qualities, making of this an object of reflection. In contrast with this uniquely human ability, animals are restricted to fulfilling needs of survival both in nature and in society (as workforce or domestic company), without reaching any higher mental status. Even if Kant acknowledges that animal behaviour demonstrates key similarities with human action, he also highlights the limitations of this analogy. For instance, the constructions of beavers mentioned in the *Critique of Judgment* (CJ 5: 464) might hint to an 'artistic capacity in animals, designated as instinct', which may be considered as an *analogon* of reason. This analogical reasoning allows understanding human behaviour as action based on representations, which groups animals with rational humans and counters arguments made by philosophers such as Descartes that considered animals mere machines.[22] In my view, this analogical link, which does not require belonging to the same species, should guide the interpretation of various Kantian statements such as the following: 'all animals are equally free' (Eth(PP)-Herder 27: 63).[23]

This distant kinship between humans and animals underpins the remark that 'a hard-heartedness towards animals is not in accordance with the law of reason.' (Eth-Vigil 27: 710). This however, should not be interpreted as recognition of a hidden overlap in the practical status of animals and humans. In fact, Kant devotes intense attention to the phenomenon he labels as 'an amphiboly in . . . concepts of reflection' (DV § 16, 6: 442), which may occur when one feels he has a duty to animals or to nature. The correct reasoning would be to view the human relation to animals as a duty 'with regard to' beings other than humans, which, ultimately, remains a duty to himself. Even if humans don't have direct duties towards animals, their duty towards themselves encourages them to cultivate sympathy and gratitude 'with regard to' animals, as animals represent an essential element of human labour while also providing pleasant company:

> With regard to the animate but nonrational part of creation, violent and cruel treatment of animals is far more intimately opposed to a human being's duty to himself, and he has a duty to refrain from this; for it dulls his shared feeling of their suffering and so weakens and gradually uproots a natural predisposition that is very serviceable to morality in one's relations with other people (DV § 17, 6: 443).

Kant also points out that treating animals with cruelty can lead to cruelty towards other humans, demonstrating the analogous role that non-rational animal beings fulfil in Kant's theory of morals.[24] Given that the animal mind is regarded as a *analogon* of the human mind, a man who, for instance, kills his

---

[22] It deserves to be mentioned that Kant compares the social status of women in the state of nature as 'a domestic animal', who 'follows [her man] loaded down with his household belongings' (Anth 7: 304). Thus in the previous stage of civilization, women are depicted as members of a human herd, still unprotected through institutions such as monogamic marriage while also not provided with the right to run a household.

[23] See for instance the interpretation of this statement by Salgueiro (2024: 11): 'This statement implies that Kant recognizes a form of freedom in animals that is analogous to human freedom, albeit limited by their natural instincts'.

[24] See Pybus and Broadie (1974: 382).

dog when it is no longer productive for him, 'is by no means in breach of any duty to the dog, since the latter is incapable of judgement, but he thereby damages the kindly and humane qualities in himself, which he ought to exercise in virtue of his duties to mankind' (Eth-Collins 27: 459). Humans should perceive animals as helpful cooperators which not only improve productivity but also our well-being, an appreciation which decidedly prohibits slaughtering them with pain, treating them with cruelty, abusing of their capacities, or torturing them in scientific experiments, which, indeed, should only be developed 'for the sake of speculation' (DV § 16, 6: 443).[25] Even if animals are not proper members of the human moral community, which does not admit non-rational animals, they are members of a teleological community, in which they perform helpful tasks on behalf of humans. In Kant's view, this instrumental contribution to human culture, in the form of animal labour or kinship must be recognized as a commitment that the rational human being adopts out of respect to his own moral principles.[26] Furthermore, Kant sees a connection between the human treatment of animals and the cultivation of humanity in general, as our approach to animals is indicative of our behaviour towards our fellow humans. Hence, our interactions with animals are a way to train our moral consciousness, which Kant supports with historical examples of condemnation of cruelty to animals, seen as a conduct that demeans the value of the subject who commits such an act:

> Any action whereby we may torment animals, or let them suffer distress, or otherwise treat them without love, is demeaning to ourselves. It is inhuman, and contains an analogy of violation of the duty to ourselves, since we would not, after all, treat ourselves with cruelty; we stifle the instinct of humaneness within us and make ourselves devoid of feeling; it is thus an indirect violation of humanity in our own person. In Athens it was punishable to let an aged work-horse starve. In England, likewise, all cruelty to animals is forbidden

---

[25] As members of the household or of the patrimony of a family, Kant's approach to animals might be compared to his understanding of the social role of domestic servants, who also cooperate to increase the well-being of the household. Naturally, domestic servants are human beings and not animals. Yet Kant intends that they become by contract an acquisition of the head of a family and thus agree '*to do whatever is permissible* for the welfare of the household' (DR 6: 360–361), as they work for satisfying the needs and guaranteeing the welfare of the family members, including women, who are relieved from the burden of child rearing by nurses and cooks. Kant fosters the legal improvement of the working status of servants, as they were traditionally treated as slaves (DR § 30, 6: 283) by suggesting what he views as 'a new star' in the normative space, that is, a right to a person akin to a right to a thing. See Pascoe (2022: 11, 18, 26) and Sánchez Madrid (2024).

[26] See Eth-Collins 27: 459: 'The more we devote ourselves to observing animals and their behavior, the more we love them, on seeing how greatly they care for their young; in such a context, we cannot even contemplate cruelty to a wolf.'

under punishment; it is recognized, therefore, that in this there is something improper, which at least can render us immoral (Eth-Vigil 27: 710).

In similar texts, Kant also references engravings by Williams Hogarth titled 'The Four Stages of Cruelty' (1751), which illustrate the progression of violent and cruel behaviour, as a helpful pedagogical tool for educating children to interact properly with humans and non-rational animals. In fact, the respect that humans are expected to show in their pragmatic interactions with animals fulfils the role of educating humans in the attitude they should adopt towards their equals, including animals and nature. In the *Lecture on Ethics Collins,* Kant discusses animals as 'an analogue of humanity', which argues for considering animal cooperation and service as merits deserving a reward comprehensible to the animal mind. Other recommendations regarding animals seem to point to the cultivation of duties to humanity, which not only refer to other humans, but also to other living beings on earth and even the natural resources which enable the survival of the human species.[27] As the following passage confirms, the legitimate use of analogical reasoning between human and animal actions reduces animal life to a sort of supplement of humanity, insofar as human beings require the cooperation of other living beings:

> If a dog, for example, has served his master long and faithfully, that is an analogue of merit; hence I must reward it, and once the dog can serve no longer, must look after him to the end, for I thereby cultivate my duty to humanity, as I am called upon to do; so if the acts of animals arise out of the same principium from which human actions spring, and the animal actions are analogues of this, we have duties to animals, in that we thereby promote the cause of humanity (Eth-Collins 27: 459).

In this way, the commitment to the moral perfection of human beings is not completely indifferent to their interactions with animals, whose suffering she has a duty to prevent and diminish. Kant also underlines the fact that human beings are able to recognize when animals feel pain or distress. Put differently, because the human mind is able to empathize with the pain of animals, he is also committed to the lifelong maintenance of the animals he may have profited from. Even if the bonds between humans and animals are mostly pragmatic and instrumental, the human being should exert a tutelary responsibility towards animals, averting the squandering and misuse of their vitality.

---

[27] See Salgueiro (2024: 18): 'While Kant significantly denies that we have any direct duties to animals (MS 6: 442), he also maintains that we have indirect duties to them, based on our own humanity and moral rationality. The moral game is a hypothetical scenario in which rational beings act according to the categorical imperative and cooperate for the sake of their humanity.' Salgueiro (2024: 23) also points out that '[d]eep anthropocentrism is incompatible with moral perfection', a remark that I fully concur with. Cfr. Müller (2022: 66).

3.2 Kant on Mental Disorder: Personal Responsibility or Tragic Misfortune?

The reasons for Kant's more sympathetic stance towards non-rational animals than towards the mentally ill deserve addressing. We must keep in mind that in eighteenth-century Germany and other European countries, people with mental disorders did not elicit compassion or sympathy, as both institutions and common sense viewed them as a charge that the rest of the community had to care for. In this vein, we cannot reasonably expect that Kant would be immune to such a commonly accepted opinion about human failure allegedly rooted in mental illness. Moreover, the medical approach at the time to such conditions left a lot to be desired, which leads Kant to argue against the confinement of these persons in asylums as was common during this era.

Kant manifested an overt interest in the causes and potential cures for mental disorders, at least since the pre-critical writing *An Essay on the Maladies of the Head* (1764). In his view, philosophers would be better equipped than physicians for inspecting the disturbed mind, particularly in the case of mental disorders in their early stages. In fact, Kant states that the philosopher could provide service for the mentally ill without requiring fees in exchange (MH 2: 271), as he views this as a sort of civil service. Already in the pre-critical period, Kant pondered potential treatments for the mentally ill, concluding that labelling and diagnosing 'the frailties of the head' (MH 2: 260) would be helpful insofar as it could allow society 'to recognize these loathsome maladies in their gradual origination' (MH 2: 260), while also taking into account their prevalence both in society and in isolation. As he does later in the *Anthropology from a Pragmatic Point of View* (1798), Kant posits in 1764 that there are two main categories of mental disorders. The first group conserves the use of understanding to some degree, so that phantasies can be managed through judgement or reason. The second group, however, has completely lost the capacity to grasp any rational argument, and moreover, appealing to reason with these subjects might be 'extremely detrimental' (MH 2: 270).

Kant develops his mature exploration of the abilities, weaknesses, and illnesses of the central epistemic faculty of the human mind in the published *Anthropology*. The evolution of this account can be also traced throughout the sequence of *Lectures on Anthropology*, in notes taken by Kant's students over decades. The defects of the cognitive faculty are thus divided into two groups: melancholia/hypochondria and sheer mental derangement manifesting in different types of mania. The first, melancholia, makes the subject aware of the imaginary diseases he falsely believes to suffer, yet he is unable to get rid of this feeling. Kant seems to commiserate with the unfortunate destiny of the individual suffering from this sort of disorder, as he 'will never really be happy in life' (Anth 7: 213). In this vein, suicide is mentioned, but only as 'the effect of a *raptus*' (Anth § 50, 7: 213) common in victims of mental disorder. Kant also hints to the human mind's power to control morbid feelings in the third part of *The Conflict of the Faculties* (CF 7: 97–116), in which he states that those suffering from hallucinations are not deserving of compassion, given that before their affliction, these people did not apply the effort required to change their pathological mental habits. In this case, it seems that Kant views melancholic individuals as responsible for their own suffering.

Discussing the second group of mental disorders, Kant points out that these do not necessarily display sheer madness, even if they may progress to that stage. In this context, Kant focuses on the importance of determining with certainty whether one accused of a crime was in his right mind or suffering from deranged judgement or understanding when perpetrating the offense. Kant argues for assigning such a judgement to the philosopher rather than to a forensic physician. To support this argument, he references a contemporary trial that had absolved a woman from the death penalty for killing 'a child out of despair' (Anth § 51, 7: 214 f.) after the judge considered her insane. As Kant stresses, the definition of insane people does not consist in gleaning 'true conclusion from false premises' (Anth § 51, 7: 214 f.), for in such a case all criminals might be called 'insane'. Kant's account of mental disorder is in fact quite concerned about potentially blurring the boundaries between culpable individuals and subjects devoid of responsibility as a result of mental disease, viewing this as a detrimental bias for penal justice. Kant's aforementioned example, following the legal institutions and the courts of his time, confirms his view that judges had not yet developed a clear concept of the borders of human responsibility, often showing too much sympathy for the motivations and purposes of a criminal mind upon confusing it with a deranged mind. This would seem to conflict with Kant's claims that insane people be treated with pity and care, yet Kant seems to hint to the fact that only subjects suffering an incurable illness should not be punished upon committing misdeeds and crimes.

With regard to the commonwealth's social responsibility towards insane or mentally ill people, Kant claims that these individuals should retreat from society to enter hospitals and asylums, where they will not bother 'normal' social life with their pathologies. In this vein, Kant dissuades his public and readers from marrying into families with antecedents of mental disorders, emphasizing the hereditary elements of these diseases, which he considers the 'most profound degradation of humanity' (Anth § 52, 7: 214). Even if he views mental disorder as a universal pathology, there are parts of Kant's account that demand an intersectional approach able to highlight gender, class, and racial factors that might characterize the profile of some people labelled 'insane'. In this sense, women appear as the central focus of Kant's description of certain mental disorders, while the race and class of those suffering from mental illness is generally disregarded. When considering the impact of the role of culture on Kant's categories of mental disorders, it would seem that at least in some cases, a European cultural bias could lead to the labelling of certain cultural behaviours as pathological expressions of a disordered mind.[28] In any case, Kant does not further develop the relation between the diagnosis of mental illness and the anthropological experience of geographical and cultural difference beyond some scattered anthropological remarks. From what we can glean from his writings, anthropological interaction across cultures is expected to increase tolerance of foreign habits and attitudes that would be considered unacceptable for fellow citizens[29], and in turn perhaps blur the line between mental health and insanity.

As seen in his analytical chart categorizing various types of mental disorders, Kant distinguishes between disordered sensory representations and disordered judgement or reason. On the one hand, *amentia* makes the subject unable to construct a sound experience from her representations, while *dementia* apparently conforms to 'the formal laws of thought' (Anth § 52, 7: 215). In this case, however, the mind undergoes an 'unhappy delusion', insofar as it interprets glances, words and inconsequential actions as aggressions from imaginary enemies. Kant observes that amentia is particularly prevalent in women, as they are supposedly more susceptible to it due to their 'talkativeness' (Anth § 52, 7: 215).[30] Sufferers from dementia, on the other hand, are depicted as subjects that do not require institutionalization, as they do not pose a risk, insofar as they are 'concerned just with themselves' (Anth § 52, 7: 215). In this way, they are differentiated from what Kant contemptuously calls 'hospital

---

[28] Without provoking an accusation of mental derangement, but rather of bad non-European taste, the example of the Iroquois Sachem (whose name Kant writes in lowercase) is quite telling, whose adventures in Paris Kant references in the *Critique of Judgment* as an example of very different cultures. See CJ § 2 (5: 204): 'nothing in Paris pleased him [the Iroquois Sachem] better than the cook-shops'.

[29] See the role that laughing fulfils as an example of toleration of other social habits and tastes that anthropological interaction involves CJ § 54, 5: 388: 'If someone tells this story: An Indian, at the table of an Englishman in Surat, seeing a bottle of ale being opened and all the beer, transformed into foam, spill out, displayed his great amazement with many exclamations, and in reply to the Englishman's question "What is so amazing here?" answered, "I'm not amazed that it's coming out, but by how you got it all in," we laugh, and it gives us a hearty pleasure: not because we find ourselves cleverer than this ignorant person, or because of any other pleasing thing that the understanding allows us to note here, but because our expectation was heightened and suddenly disappeared into nothing.'

[30] Kant rephrases the language of *What is Enlightenment?* to laugh down the allegedly uncontrolled speech of women to argue, even in trials, in favour of the interest of their husbands, hinting to them as 'over-mature' [*übermündig*] speakers. See Anth § 48, 7: 209.

buffoons' (Anth § 52, 7: 215), a seemingly derogatory term for those needing medical and psychological assistance. Kant also addresses *insania* as a disorder resulting from 'a deranged power of imagination' (Anth § 52, 7: 215), in which the insane subject draws imaginary connections between unrelated phenomena, and *vesania*, which shows 'the sickness of a deranged *reason*' (Anth § 52, 7: 215). While *insania* makes the subject cheerful, those with *vesania* are described as self-enclosed subjects, fully bereft of common sense and isolated in the representation of their own contrived reality. Notably, they appear as 'the calmest of all hospital patients' (Anth § 52, 7: 216).

Here, we must ask whether Kant encourages feeling a sort of reflective sympathy regarding mentally ill people. In his account of mental disorder, Kant stresses the fact that the vesanic subject has devised an alternate reality, which entails a shift from common sense to a 'logical private sense' (Anth § 53, 7: 219) losing the potential for communication with others:

> [F]rom the *Sensorio communi* that is required for the unity of *life* (of the animal), it finds itself transferred to a faraway place (hence the word 'derangement' (*Verrückung*)) – just as a mountainous landscape sketched from a bird's-eye view prompts a completely different judgment about the region than when it is viewed from level ground (Anth § 52, 7: 216).

As the excerpt conveys, Kant attempts to dissect the very meaning of the German word *Verrückung*, whose traditional meaning refers to extreme mental disorder. In these insane subjects, their mental faculties do not fulfil an epistemic purpose, but rather serve simply to maintain their survival while they remain lost in a phantasy world, incapable of objectivity. To a certain extent, then, the life of the insane person is reduced to that of the animal, demeaning their humanity and making them a burden for their commonwealth. That said, Kant proceeds cautiously with regard to the institutional care of insane people. As we have seen, the pathological human mind appears radically excluded from the emotional and epistemic human community, in contrast with the 'humanisation' of animals in return for the aid and company they provide humans. Furthermore, Kant holds that even milder mental pathologies represent *epistemic bubbles* making the mentally disordered subject unable to compare their private judgements with the rules guiding our representations to acquire a universal value. Yet Kant also neglects the possibility of care required to treat different mental disorders, deeming this issue pragmatically unimportant for his account of mental derangement and illness. Put slightly differently, Kant's sympathetic approach to non-human or non-rational living beings seems not to apply to the case of mental insanity, as the epistemic isolation of insane people deprives them of the recognition human beings show to non-human domesticated animals. In some cases, in Kant's view, the blame for mental disorder falls on the negligence of the subject, while in others, it appears hereditary, but still undeserving of compassion. Yet, as mentioned at the onset of this subsection, Kant's approach to mental disorder could not be interpreted without considering the ideological framework of his time. Thus, it would unfair to blame assign Kant the responsibility for not considering the social inclusion of mentally ill people a moral duty. Put differently, Kant was deeply under the influence of a quite utilitarian account of social membership, which was unable to conceive of the potential contributions of the mentally ill to the commonwealth, for instance, in proposing different perspectives on reality. Kant's harsh approach to mental illness, however, does not relinquish society's responsibility to care for these subjects through public and private asylums and hospitals, as the commonwealth has a duty not to aggravate the degradation of the humanity they embody.

4 Poverty Relief and Social Suffering

Kant does not address the poor individual as one who has been thwarted by failed endeavours. Rather, Kant's view of the poor has two aspects: he highlights the passivity of these members of the commonwealth that makes them a social burden, while simultaneously presenting them as the victims of forgotten or denied injustices.[31] Correct interpretation of such an ambiguous account is challenging, and must be analysed by addressing the central features of both aspects of Kant's account: the suspicion of laziness underpinning poverty, on the one hand, and the victimhood of the poor resulting from public injustices on the other. It bears repeating that Kant's account of dignity, closely related to the goal of moral autonomy, guides his reasoning bearing on the problem of poverty, while also showcasing blatant shortcomings in his reasoning that would lead to practices unacceptable in modern society.

Having discussed the weaknesses of Kant's account of poverty relief, in the next subsections I will analyse the contrast between the abstract approach to

---

[31] In contrast with the hesitations showed in the case of poverty, Kant blatantly denounces the violence and cruelty that colonialism unleashes in other continents, as embodied by the Sugar Islands slave trade (PP 8: 359). I do not focus on this barbarous effect of colonialism as a political pathology, for in my view, Kant does not address the proper response of each individual state in grappling with this abhorrence. While poverty radically challenges state sovereignty, colonialism displays, in Kant's view, an exploitation and domination that drags down the political international order, and which requires the cooperation of all 'civilized' nations to remedy. See on this issue Kleingeld (2014: 52–58) and the more critical account by Lu-Adler (2022: 280–284). I am thankful to Jordan Fascoe for drawing my attention to the fact that Kant's criticism of chattel slavery sheds light on his intention to see the ensuing suffering as either structurally produced or potentially shaped by the will of states responsible for ending such a breach of international law.

this social pathology and another more concrete one, as textual evidence of both can be found. While the first line of analysis tends to view economic hardship as a challenge for the conservation of the citizenry as a whole, the second blames individuals for economic injustice, especially the descendants of those who committed economic abuses in the past. Thus, Kant focuses on poverty from two different points of view, that is, as a social emergency concerning the public power and as a moral challenge for economically independent people. Moreover, this double outlook also entails two different reactions towards the breach of human dignity underpinning the phenomenon of poverty.

One conspicuous limitation of this account of poverty relief is the absence of direct testimony from the poor[32], who are consistently addressed as passive sectors of the commonwealth unable to attain economic independence and thus become potential active citizens. A second limitation is the way that Kant charges wealthy citizens with the duty to support the poor in order to preserve the commonwealth. A third limitation is Kant's reluctance to promote direct legislative intervention to prevent increasing numbers of people from falling into poverty because of their inability to climb out of debt. Kant views economic failure not as the result of any structural injustice, but rather the subject's inability to succeed within a classical liberal market struggling to transition away from aristocratic privilege (Sánchez Madrid 2018).

Kant's account of the tragedy of poverty and deprivation may seem unpromising in terms of the recognition of suffering in society. That said, in this section, I will aim to provide an interpretation of Kant in which the public has a responsibility to mitigate an uncontrolled increase in economic inequality, without interrupting the normal dynamics of the liberal market. In my view, making poverty relief a public commitment to combat the threat of population contraction sets limits on unrestrained economic growth throughout the commonwealth, even if Kant does not engage into a detailed discussion of the perversions of liberal economics, which Hegel attempted to address decades later in his *Principles of the Philosophy of Right*.[33]

---

[32] Hegel will undertake more compassionate approach to the poor as a social and civil failure. See Hegel, GPhR § 242: 188: 'The *subjective* aspect of poverty, and in general of every kind of want to which all individuals are exposed, even in their natural environment, also requires subjective help, both with regard to the particular circumstances and with regard to *emotion* and *love*. This is a situation in which, notwithstanding all universal arrangements, *morality* finds plenty to do.' According to Kant morality must withdraw precisely for the sake of settling the social challenge of poverty.

[33] See Hegel, GPhR § 244: 189: 'The important question of how poverty can be remedied is one which agitates and torments modern societies especially.'

4.1 Does Poverty Constitute Social Suffering in Kant's View?

There has been much scholarship (Weinrib 2003; Gilabert 2010; Allais 2014; Baiasu 2014; Sánchez Madrid 2018, 2019; Holtman 2018; Loriaux 2020; Davies 2023; Pinzani 2023; Blöser 2023) devoted to addressing Kant's account of poverty as a critical phenomenon endangering the stability of the civil commonwealth required for preservation of the citizenry as a whole.[34] The aim of this subsection, however, will be to inspect whether Kant views poverty as damaging to the confidence the subject has in her own ability. While Kant advocates for social meritocracy over the privileges of a parasitic aristocracy, he seems oblivious to the harmful effects of adversity and misery on the humanity of those who suffer from it, particularly that poverty often undermines the poor's consciousness of their civil duty. It appears that in Kant's view, the poor must always ask himself what he can do for the commonwealth, rather than demanding help and support from it. As Flikschuh points out in her interpretation of Kant's theory of the state, an understanding of the specific aspects of the liberal approach that Kant endorses in his political philosophy is crucial (Flikschuh 2010: 69). In this account of political authority, metaphysical structures take priority over the demands of individuals, who would be unable to form any sort of civil union by simply gathering their bodies and demands.[35]

Yet alternative readings of poverty relief as a public duty may be derived from Kant's legal and political philosophy, as some of the interpreters mentioned argue for (Weinrib 2003: 795–801; Gilabert 2010: 411–413; Loriaux 2020: 28–34; Blöser 2023: 294–297). Usually, these different accounts highlight that Kant does not disavow that poor people may 'work [their] way up' with the help of their effort and capacities to fulfil an active role for the commonwealth, as they have not lost their ability to support themselves especially if the state helps them to attain it. Generally, such readings hinge on the organicism underpinning Kant's notion of the commonwealth, which claims a full-fledged reciprocity of means and ends among its social members. Moreover, Kant's vision of an idealized liberal market does not easily lend itself to perceiving the obstacles posed by inequality and exploitation that cause economic hardship for countless people. The following well-known excerpt

---

[34] Some interpreters see poverty as a global concern that embraces the perception of the poor, which I consider a Kantian-inspired reading, rather than an impartial account of Kant's theses. See Blöser (2023: 300): 'From a Kantian point of view, the insight that the poor need more hope must go hand in hand with a commitment to establishing trustworthy structures, such that their hope can be rational'.

[35] Baiasu (2014: 25f.) apropos highlights Kant's *Reflexion* 8000 (Refl 19: 578), which states that poverty relief does not stem from the rights of the poor as citizens, but from their needs as human beings, which seems to demand specific protection in Kant's political philosophy.

from the writing *Theory and Practice* provides a fruitful point of departure for discussing Kant's remarks on poverty as a political concern:

> [A human being] can be considered happy ... provided he is aware that, if he does not reach the same level as others, the fault lies only in himself ([his lack of] ability or earnest will) or circumstances for which he cannot blame any other, but not in the irresistible will of others who, as his fellow subjects in this condition, have no advantage over him as far as right is concerned (TP, 8: 293–294).

Despite the many hurdles stemming from economic and social inequality, which force him to recognize a difference between passive and active citizenship, Kant truly believes 'that anyone can work his way up from [the] passive condition to an active one' (DR § 46, 6: 315).[36] However, he neither enquires which means would best assist the subject in undertaking such a task nor how best to aid him in his struggle for social recognition.[37] Thus, the reasons for the success or failure of individuals attempting to reach higher economic strata remain quite puzzling, insofar as there is nothing other than the market for labour and goods in which one can exhibit their capacities and merits. Along with this analysis of economic inequality, which Kant ascribes to the imbalance in inherited wealth stemming from a forgotten 'original accumulation', he also addresses the reaction of the state towards the increase in poverty as a social crisis. As the state embodies the *universal will* of a civil union, which does not overlap with that of society,[38] Kant clearly neglects the individual experience of poverty – a demeaning situation that deprives the subject of his own autonomy – focusing rather on highlighting the social crisis the state must resolve. He tackles this issue precisely in a sequence of sections where he examines the attributes of the lawgiver in extreme, controversial, and uncertain circumstances. In this context, Kant reminds us that:

> The general will of the people has united itself into a society which is to maintain itself perpetually; and for this end it has submitted itself to the internal authority of the state in order to maintain those members of the society who are unable to maintain themselves. For reasons of state the government is therefore authorized to constrain the wealthy to provide the means of sustenance to those who are unable to provide for even their most necessary natural needs. The wealthy have acquired an obligation to the

---

[36] Hasan (2018: 925) considers that, while TP does not address a statist agenda against economic inequality, DR engages into a more accurate reflection on it, as it views it as a threat to full-fledged external freedom.

[37] I give a more detailed account of Kant's rejection of any duty of the state to help the citizens to improve their social status in Sánchez Madrid (2018, 2019). See a defence of a Kantian 'duty of right to combat poverty' in Loriaux (2020: 28–34). See also Holtman on poverty relief as a public burden (Holtman 2018: 58–60).

[38] See DR § 41, 6: 306–307 on the distinction between the horizontal meaning of *society* and the hierarchical structure ingrained in *civil union*.

commonwealth, since they owe their existence to an act of submitting to its protection and care, which they need in order to live; on this obligation the state now bases its right to contribute what is theirs to maintaining their fellow citizens (DR 6: 325–326).

This excerpt allows focusing on the public authority of the lawgiver grounded in Kant's legal and political philosophy, in which the economic power of some citizens is put under the control of the lawgiver. This representative of the united will of the nation may force the wealthy to guarantee the basic maintenance of those incapable of attaining any economic autonomy.[39] Thus, the lawgiver must consider the needs of the citizenry as a whole in order to prevent eventual discord and upheaval, even if this economic support does not entail providing civil self-sufficiency to outcast members of society. Moreover, poverty relief will be enacted by the imposition of taxes on property or economic activity, or by public foundations providing assistance to the least fortunate members of society. Here, Kant openly argues for public funds to combat poverty, as he considers that donations often seek to profit off of the attention devoted to the poor, contributing to impoverishment among groups that were previously unaffected by this scourge.[40] Moreover, he points out that the suggested measures should not constitute a parasitic relationship with active citizens. Put differently, Kant stresses the need to prevent care for the poor from becoming a perpetual state, which would both stifle the self-respect of the impoverished while also illegitimately burdening the self-sufficient part of the citizenry.[41] Kant claims that the state's imposition of 'legal levies' on wealthy people, so that each generation can support 'its own poor' (DR 6: 326) is a bothersome burden, predicting that the beneficiaries of this economic aid might decide to stop trying to 'work their own way up', which would in turn inhibit the correct functioning of society.[42] On the

---

[39] See Baiasu (2014: 23): 'Kant does not talk about welfare in terms of duties or rights; he only talks about the state's right or authorisation to tax the wealthy.' Davies points out the question of the conditions poor people would have to meet for receiving public support (Davies 2020: 19–20), as Kant aims to prevent that 'poverty [becomes] a means of acquisition for the lazy' (DR 6: 326).

[40] See Weinrib on Kant's foundation of the public commitment to poverty relief (2003: 820): 'Because the state is under a duty, it has no discretion to withhold the support; and having no private interest of its own, it also has no motivation to withhold support. The receipt of state support thus does not make the needy subservient to the will of others'. See a similar interpretation in Ripstein (2009: 282).

[41] On this point, see Loriaux (2023: 246): 'Underlying the Prussian welfare state of the eighteenth century was the idea that public aid must not encourage laziness, but must, as far as possible, give the poor the means to provide for themselves, and thereby ensure that they are no longer a burden for the public or a source of crimes.'

[42] Kant does not consider that the state should provide civil self-sufficiency to the whole population, as such a goal would constitute a paternalistic cameralist agenda (Loriaux 2020: 25–26), which views the natural resources and economic progress of a nation under teleological principles controlled by the public authority. Gilabert (2010: 412–413) also stresses Kant's rejection of any paternalism as he addresses poverty relief.

same token, private pious and religious institutions should be averted given their potential to contribute to political paternalism, which threatens to spoil the individual initiative to overcome social obstacles.[43]

Given that in this context, happiness is understood as the result of individual success in the classical liberal market, following Adam Smith's proposals, Kant does not attend to the pain and frustration inherent to the experience of poverty, which makes the impoverished completely dependent on the charity of 'private' others. The opposite of the impoverished subject, in Kant's view, is the self-sufficient man, who has the wealth and property to fund his existence and has no master other than the commonwealth itself.[44] In this sense, Kant assumes that an interdependence between individuals and their societal standing underpins the commonwealth and the understanding of civil self-sufficiency (Vrousalis 2022). Although only successful businessmen, civil officers, and independent workers may expect to be considered co-legislators, no human must be excluded in Kant's account of citizenship, even if he cannot demonstrate active civil membership due to his lack of economic self-sufficiency. That said, the suffering of poor people is never the focus of this approach to social vulnerability, instead, they are consistently rebuked and blamed for missed actions and opportunities able to rectify their present circumstances.[45] Kant does, however, recommend that wealthy benefactors not humiliate the needy out of respect for their value as humans (DR § 23, 6: 448–449). In this vein, it is helpful to dissect a reflection on the dark side of the classical virtue of magnanimity, praised by Aristotle in his *Nicomachean Ethics*. In this passage, Kant views magnanimity as a threat to ascribing to any authority other than the will of the wealthy benefactor:

> Many people take pleasure in doing good actions but consequently do not want to stand under obligations toward others. If one only comes to them submissively, they will do everything: they do not want to subject themselves to the rights of people, but to view them simply as objects of magnanimity. It is not all one under what title I get something. What properly belongs to me must not be accorded to me merely as something I beg for (Refl 19: 145).

This tension between the virtue of beneficence and the legal demands for public assistance to society's neediest individuals pervades Kant's account of poverty

---

[43] See an account of a Kant-inspired agenda to alleviate global poverty going beyond the remit of the particular states in Loriaux (2020: 45–56).

[44] To dissect Kant's civil self-sufficiency Davies (2023: 124) suggests adopting an 'authority reading' of it, which nevertheless could also be considered as a corollary of what he labels as the 'economic readings' (Pinzani and Sánchez Madrid 2016) of this principle of Kantian republicanism.

[45] Mieth and Williams suggest a novel interpretation of Kant's practical and political philosophy, insofar as they highlight the key moral and political task to contribute to enlarge the opportunities to be considered 'useful members of the world' in birth or host societies. See Mieth and Williams (2021).

and the duty of the ruler of the state to relieve it before it becomes a threat to society. I will address this in the next subsection. Although Kant's remarks on poor people lack any solidarity and compassion in a contemporary sense, he does consider it demeaning for the poor to have to beg in the streets, rendering them dependent of the charity of others. In this sense, the beggar appears as the opposite of the individual who fulfils the duties of self-esteem as a rational and moral being. In fact, Kant even compares begging to robbery (DR 6: 326), as seen in the key passage quoted above. Furthermore, in the *Lecture on Ethics Vigilantius*, Kant affirms that the beggar depreciates 'his personhood' and with such a behaviour 'displays the highest degree of contempt for himself' (Eth-Vigil 27: 605), requiring the state to intervene as the primary supporter of the poor. Taking into account such excerpts, interpreters such as Allais argue for overcoming the limitations of charity and beneficence through the statist decision to intervene in order to appease the self-destructive cycle which traps the needy within the societally competitive space.[46] Despite the evidently disparate reasoning of the *Doctrine of Right* and the *Lectures on Ethics*, it is also clear that public measures to alleviate poverty do not relinquish individual responsibility with regard to other human beings. Moreover, Kant's awareness of the material conditions needed to exercise and concretize freedom[47] does not demonstrate a discourse sympathetic with the demands that poor people might raise. On the contrary, the supreme commander of the civil union is entitled to obligate well off citizens to mitigate the damage that marginalized people cause for the commonwealth, without ever convening these vulnerable social groups to hear their complaints and hopes. Such a resistance against giving a voice to marginalized people outlines some limitations of Kant's social imagination, which tends to reject the idea that vulnerable people may act as bearers of moral and political authority and thus help more advantaged subjects to enlarge their moral perception.[48]

---

[46] See Allais (2014: 18): 'If there are genuine beggars, then there is structural injustice of a sort which makes it impossible for you to relate rightfully to these individuals in individual encounters'. See also Eth-Collins, 27: 456: 'Alms-giving is a form of kindness associated with pride and costing no trouble, and a beneficence calling for no reflection. Men are demeaned by it. It would be better to think out some other way of assisting such poverty, so that men are not brought so low as to accept alms'. See also Holtman (2018: 61–63).

[47] Pinzani suggests justifying a UBI according to Kantian tenets, based on the imperative to maintain the *civitas*. See Pinzani (2023: 235): '[I]t is possible to shift from the dominant liberal reading of Kant's concept of freedom toward a more nuanced interpretation in which the formal character of this concept does not exclude the existence of material conditions that need to be satisfied if individuals are to maintain their innate freedom.'

[48] I am thankful to Garrath Williams for alerting me to the importance of this gap in Kant's evaluation of social and economic problems for interpreting the contemporary value of his moral theory and social philosophy. For more on this matter, see Russel (2020: 281–282) and Schaab (2021: 509–511).

4.2 The Moral Instinct to Alleviate the Effects of the 'Injustice of the Government'

Kant's account of poverty yields quite deceptive conclusions for interpreters searching for an argument for poverty relief based on compassion towards those living in vulnerable situations. Yet I would like to address, in this subsection, Kant's call to the responsibility of all active citizens in alleviating the disfavoured situation of economically vulnerable members of the same commonwealth. As seen previously, Kant emphasizes that marginalized people belong to a commonwealth that the supreme commander is committed to protect, legitimating him to decide to tax wealthy citizens in order to maintain the worst off members of society. However, this decision stemming from the will of protecting the state and embodied in its population, does not guarantee active civil membership to the social groups benefitting from this assistance, as it is only the obligation to protect the commonwealth from any internal or external threat that guides this rationale. Thus, the social and civil advancement of individuals does not belong to this agenda, as such an advancement can only be realized by the efforts of these subjects themselves. Yet Kant discusses another aspect of economic inequality which directly addresses the personal responsibility of individual subjects, awakening their awareness of their complicity in historical injustices that their governments may have committed in the past and which might have become naturalized in the present. Kant's view of beneficence, understood as the flipside of self-love, that is, 'our need to be loved (helped in case of need) by others as well' (DV 6: 393), is a key element in Kant's struggle against unjust economic inequality. Put slightly differently, Kant views the happiness of others as an aim guaranteeing that we also will be, if necessary, 'an end for others' (DV 6: 393).[49]

The *Lecture on Ethics Vigilantius*, which focuses on the application of morals to practical life, also demonstrates this structure of interdependence underpinning Kant's view of duty to others[50]. It dismisses adopting, as a maxim, 'indifference to the suffering and needs of others' (Eth-Vigil § 12, 27: 496),

---

[49] See Baron and Fahmy (2009: 220): '[T]he duty of beneficence is not reducible to a duty to aid only those in desperate need, but rather should be understood more broadly to include assisting others with personal projects and endeavors.' Cfr Baron (1995: 39–52). See the normative account of beneficence in Kant as 'a moderately demanding conception of beneficence' in Formosa and Sticker (2019: 637), who highlight the fact that Kant urges conflating the fulfilment of ethical duties with developing personal practical projects.

[50] See Holtman (2018: 71): '[R]esponsibilities of justice in the realm of social welfare have their source not in the self-focused aims of individuals or even in a more outward-looking concern to prevent deception or unjustified coercion. Instead, such responsibilities are founded in an agency that is both personal and joint and whose successful development and exercise requires the support of each and all.'

even if an individual might fulfil his aims without considering his commitment to alleviate the material needs of the vulnerable.[51] This again relates to the *Doctrine of Virtue*, particularly to the fact that every finite rational being might, at some point, require 'the assistance of others' as he 'may fall into a similarly needy condition' (Eth-Vigil § 12, 27: 496). These excerpts provide textual evidence of the claim that Kant grounds his universal moral obligations on human vulnerability, seeking a system able to safeguard citizens from potential misfortunes. Put differently, an allegedly universal maxim of social indifference towards the suffering of others would not be in the best interest of anyone, insofar as all individuals are characterized by human frailty and the potential to be beset by future misfortune.[52]

Just as this possibility of misfortune and indigence argues for a moral duty to assist others, Kant also shows misgivings towards an overly enthusiastic realization of this obligation, which might risk the wealth and welfare of entire families. In this vein, Kant discusses the limits of the broad duty to provide assistance to others in need, stating that this does not command 'determinate actions' (DV 6: 393). In this way, prudence in the practice of beneficence must orient its realization in society. Beyond the proper exercise of duties towards others, Kant states that potentially beneficent (normally wealthy) people, should not boast about their donations and benefactions, revelling in their own generosity, insofar as their action responds to 'the injustice of the government' (DV § 31, 6: 454). This aforementioned public injustice is assumed to have benefited the ancestors of the presently wealthy class, while simultaneously harming the ancestors of those now poor. In this way, the subject feeling he has carried out a meritorious duty by sharing part of his wealth with the poor is admonished to view his action as a rectification of a past injustice in which he is at least somewhat complicit.[53]

---

[51] On the value of human interdependence see Loriaux (2020: 8): '[A] human being cannot will the maxim of indifference to hold as a universal law because they cannot coherently will being deprived of the help that may prove necessary to achieve their necessary ends.' Cfr. O'Neill (1989: 348, 354).

[52] Kant's 'sense of injustice' thus takes a very different approach than that Shklar made to social responsibility and public justice, as this political theorist decided to centre the discussion around the standpoint of victims, which Kant never focuses on. In this vein, Shklar argues that the boundaries between injustice and misfortune are often fuzzy (see Shklar 1990: 55–65). Cfr. Young's suggestion to adopt a 'social connection model of injustice' in Young (2011: 171–187).

[53] Moving from these texts from the DV and the *Lectures on Ethics*, Pinheiro Walla suggests to break analysing two intertwined sides of justice in Kant (2019: 6), which blur the boundaries between moral and political philosophy, insofar as they show that the moral action of an individual can have impact on the civil advancement of others: 'Kant claims that one can take a share in general injustice, in a way that does not presuppose the violation of any specific laws of the state. In other words, it is possible to do wrong without doing any form of injustice identifiable by the system of laws. Kant's claim presupposes two different concepts of justice and injustice: one that can be recognised with reference to the positive laws of the state and one which cannot be recognised from a positive legal perspective.'

The *Lecture on Ethics Collins* provides key remarks regarding the interdependence of the duties of goodwill, embodied in the duty of benevolence,[54] and the duties of indebtedness, relying on the respect of the subject towards the sacred 'rights of others' (Eth-Collins 27: 415). Even if '[t]he right of the other should keep him secure in everything [as] it is stronger than any bulwark or wall' (Eth-Collins 27: 415), Kant also addresses the 'instinct of benevolence', which he understands as a feeling inserted by Providence into the human heart to aid in the fulfilment of moral actions. It is this moral instinct – not for justice, but rather for benevolence – that will make the human being willing to rectify an injustice that may have benefited him or that he may have unwittingly performed:

> By this impulse men take pity on another, and render back the benefits they have previously snatched away, though they are not aware of any injustice; the reason being, that they do not rightly examine the matter (Eth-Collins 27: 415).

This passage shows Kant's account of justice in its fullest form, as the natural propensity to be kind and bountiful with others results in beneficent actions. That said, Kant emphasizes that such actions, once carried out, should not be ascribed to the moral quality of the doer, as he would have 'repaid [the benefited] what [he had] helped to take away through a general injustice' (Eth-Collins 27: 415–416). Later in these sections, Kant stresses that had individual subjects reflected on the rights of others before retaining 'more of this world's goods than his neighbour' (Eth-Collins 27: 415–416) there would not be such a yawning chasm between the rich and poor of the commonwealth. In fact, this double-sided account of justice reveals the priority of the rights of other citizens with respect to the rights of the wealthy, which often arise from past injustices, that is, the original division of land. Nevertheless, as mentioned above, Kant is also concerned about the destructive impact that the instinct of benevolence might have on property rights. Therefore, he dissuades acting systematically 'from benevolence merely', as this would risk the property titles already authorized by the public power of the state. Furthermore, were benevolence to reign in society, all competition would vanish due to an alleged naturalization of luxury:

> [T]he world would be a stage, not of reason, but of inclination, and nobody would trouble to earn anything, but would rely on the charity of others. In that case, however, there would have to be the greatest abundance of everything,

---

[54] On the distinction between the duty of benevolence and the duty of beneficence, see Loriaux (2020: 13): 'Given that beneficence, unlike mere benevolence, requires *doing* something, it cannot possibly be without limits. We can certainly wish the happiness of *all* others, but by our external actions, we can only advance the happiness of *some* others. We cannot but miss some occasions to help or do good to others. Kant also admits that once external actions, and not merely wishes, are at stake, the degree of beneficence may vary according to the diversity of the persons who are loved'.

and it would all be passive, as when children enjoy something which one of them shares out to the rest, so long as it lasts (Eth-Collins 27: 416–417).

This 'shadowy' image portrays one of the most dreadful phantasies in Kant's view: 'the empty longing of a self-defeating Golden Age' (CB 8: 122–123). In this situation, civilization decays because there is no need to make an effort or work to obtain material benefits or moral progress. Kant suggests that moralists and teachers be careful in preaching such acts of kindness, as he understands that good sense and measure should guide the education in benevolence.[55] In this way, from the point of view of the agent, the broad duty towards others entails some threats. Kant's account of benevolence also addresses the impossibility of enforcing the accomplishment of benevolent actions, at least insofar as they are not reformulated as a mandatory measure issued by the 'supreme commander' (DR 6: 325) of the commonwealth. Moreover, these kinds of actions belong to a special type of right, that is, *equity*, which can enforce *coram foro interno*, but not *coram foro externo*, insofar as one's conscience is internal and private (Eth-Collins 27: 433). In sum, while Kant does not discard the fact that the moral consciousness of citizens might influence the perception they have of the suffering of others, he considers that there is a limitation of the ability of moral duties to shape relations among individuals.

Although both the instinct of benevolence, and the exercise of it, might lead to unduly disrespecting the rights of other citizens out of concern for marginalized people, Kant demonstrates the key role of moral education in cultivating a sound awareness of social injustice and how individuals might rectify it. To begin with, he reproaches the subject who first ensures that all his own material needs are met, 'and thereafter thinks to pay off their tribute to the benefactor by giving something to the poor' (Eth-Collins 27: 455). If educators could help to change this egoistic mindset, Kant assures that poverty could be eradicated from our societies – individual agents would be more conscientious in their actions, as opposed to simply donating their excess wealth to needy people, demeaning them in the process.[56] Moreover, this approach to benevolence touches on the fact that individuals should inquire within as to whether they have partaken 'in public and general oppressions' (Eth-Collins 27: 432), which would render a donation not an act of spontaneous kindness, but rather the rectification of a prior misdeed.

---

[55] See Eth-Collins 27: 456: 'Many moralists try to soften our hearts, and to commend kind acts done from tenderness; but true good actions come from sturdy souls, and to be virtuous a man must be staunch.'

[56] The large scope Kant assigns to this awareness of global injustices committed in the past is very visible in the *Lecture on Ethics Collins*. See Eth-Collins, 27: 456: 'Beneficence to others must rather be commended as a debt we owe, than as a piece of kindness and generosity; and so it is in fact; for all acts of kindness are but small repayments of our indebtedness.'

At the same time, Kant condemns the willingness of the subject to be beneficent, as this leads to the loss of his own property and economic position, thus contravening their own rights. Kant's moral philosophy thus encourages the individual agent to contribute, prudently, to restoring justice in contexts and situations requiring improvement.[57] Thus, the exercise of benevolence, as in the case of other moral virtues towards others, should not jeopardize the economic status of the donor, or as previously mentioned, generate more poverty in its attempt to offset present precarity. Perhaps, for this reason, Kant decided in the *Doctrine of Right* to accord the state decisive agency for intervening in the social crises of precarity and indigence. As seen in this section, this account does not focus on the victims of poverty and indigence, as their voices and demands are not directly addressed. Nevertheless, maintaining the subsistence of the poor becomes a duty both for the lawgiver and the individual citizen, although their power of intervention remains quite unequal.

5 Kant on the Social Suffering of Women

As is well known, Kant did not hold sympathetic attitudes towards the advancement of women in society, openly reducing them to a passive element of the commonwealth. That said, this section will inspect the extent to which he reflected on certain sources of suffering and oppression that primarily concern the socially dependent roles of women. I suggest exploring two telling cases bearing on the obstacles facing Prussian women in eighteenth century. I will first address questions posed to Kant by a woman likely suffering from mental illness in the hopes of obtaining therapeutic guidance from the author of a *Critique of Practical Reason*. Second, I will parse out the difference between moral and penal judgement of unwed mothers. Both cases exhibit women's vulnerability in a highly patriarchal and oppressive society in which they were only valued for their sexual honour. Furthermore, the civil standing of women appears as a thorny issue in Kant's anthropological and political philosophy (Varden 2015: 30), as they are regarded as merely passive social agents despite their potential rationality, indispensable to the reproduction of households they cannot afford to maintain alone, given their lack of economic independence and alleged civil maturity (Anth 7: 303–306).

---

[57] Kant's distinction between *beneficence* and *justice* hints to the classical distinction that Cicero argues for in *De officiis*, 2.16: '[A]s, on the one hand, we secure great advantages through the sympathetic cooperation of our fellow-men; so, on the other, there is no curse so terrible but it is brought down by man upon man.' I am thankful to Angela Taraborrelli for drawing my attention to this intellectual debt with Cicero's ethics, spread in Kant's time through *Popularphilosophen* as Garve.

Considering Kant's acceptance of the misogynistic prejudices of his time, his reluctance to engage in dialogue with a mentally disordered woman is unsurprising, as he feels unable to put limits on her imagination: he references the letters of Maria von Herbert as an example of a behaviour that no woman should ever display. Yet he also stands up for unmarried mothers against persecution from both barbaric legislation and religious institutions. His remarks can be interpreted to claim that, even if women are deemed passive citizens, they should not be treated in ways that demean their dignity. In the case of Maria von Herbert, Kant interprets her concerns regarding the meaning of life and love as problems to be solved through the application of a sound moral character. That said, the commonwealth also has a duty to assist unwed mothers through the establishment of foundling homes funded by 'confirmed bachelors' of both sexes. Kant encourages civil society to undertake these measures to put an end to the tragedy of maternal infanticide, often perpetrated to conceal the moral transgression of a woman giving 'herself up to the man's desire without marriage' (Anth 7: 304).

While Kant fails in providing his admirer helpful tips to cope with the depressive emotions she was experiencing, this text does provide some useful information that warrants consideration. Notably, Kant treats this woman from a neutral point of view, putting the onus for redirecting her life on her, and confirming his view that most mental illnesses may be healed through pure force of will of those afflicted. Our philosopher prioritizes the safeguarding of illegitimate children over the social reintegration of unwed mothers, even as he crafts a moral reform able to change the perception of the civil status of these women.[58]

As seen previously, Kant does not allocate suffering women a central role in his reasoning. That said, he does advocate that the commonwealth strives to eliminate contradictions in the realms of morals and penal justice by increasing the commitment to interdependence among all its members. The author that affirmed that 'a violation of right on *one* place of the earth is felt in *all*' (PP 8: 360) shows his awareness of shared responsibility for remedying regrettable abuses and excesses, especially those perpetrated by outdated religious institutions. Nevertheless, he does not understand the subjective experience of suffering as something able to be brought under control through sheer force of will. This confirms the limitations of Kant's philosophy for mitigating structural

---

[58] The social reformer of the French Revolution, Olympe de Gouges, proposed to issue daring measures to give a full civil recognition to illegitimate children and their mothers. Kant's misgivings against the epistemic achievements of women did not foster an intellectual encounter with the transforming agenda of such a female civil leader. I am indebted with Angela Taraborrelli for hinting me to the progressive agenda in social and civil rights of women suggested by some French revolutionary reformers.

injustice, even if he conjecturally recognizes some of these unfair inequalities. Kant does not completely disregard the existence of marginalized social agents who do not seem to be able to integrate into society, but in fact devotes some sections of his legal writings to reflect on such frictions. Yet the solutions to this problem that he suggests fail to effectively help stigmatized people gain acceptance within the commonwealth, and moreover, can continue to foster oppression and domination, even when based on a foundation of social assistance for the needy. In any case, Kant might inspire interpreters to address the social maladies he felt required correcting under the lens of structural injustice.

5.1 Kant's Failure as Therapist: The Challenge of Marie von Herbert

As seen in the section devoted to mental disorder, Kant manifests an overt discomfort towards the mentally ill, who, in his view, cannot have a role in society, and suffer from an incurable derangement of the faculties of the mind. As a matter of fact, Kant did not see much value in addressing such anthropological profiles, beyond fleshing out a useful analysis of the characteristics and categories of illness. For this reason, Kant's correspondence with Maria von Herbert, a woman who sent three letters to Kant searching for solace and guidance, is interesting. Of course, Kant was not a therapist, but a bachelor living in a flourishing city in eighteenth-century Prussia, which does not bode for a very promising response to Maria von Herbert's troubles. In this subsection, I will make some conjectures regarding the reasons for Kant to leaving the last letters of this young admirer unanswered. Yet more nuanced hypotheses could be added by scholars who lay out a more comprehensive account that highlights Kant's bewilderment towards the questions that this woman set to him after having loosely read some of his writings.[59] In the letters, Kant views the arguments and issues raised by von Herbert as evidence of a deranged mind possessed by an uncontrolled imagination, and thus decided to cease contact with her, only responding to the first of the three. That said, the correspondence between von Herbert (who Kant referred to as 'the little day-dreamer' (*die kleine Schwärmerin*)) and Kant showcase Kant's demanding attitude towards his acquaintances and admirers, especially women.[60] My main aim in this

---

[59] I wish to thank one of the reviewers of this Element for suggesting me to highlight this feature of the failed dialogue between Kant and Maria von Herbert. Even if I mostly share the points made by interpreters as Langton (1992: 500–501) and Cholbi (2000: 173–176), I am also in debt with the alternative accounts of Ritter (2021: 149–154), Mahon (2006: 427–438) and Varden (2020a: 160–163).

[60] The editor of the volume of Kant's *Correspondence* in the Cambridge Edition, Arnulf Zweig, points out Kant's inconsistencies with regard to the intellectual development and social furtherance of women. See Zweig (1999: 5): 'We observe or can infer Kant's ambivalence about the

section will be determining what (if any) role suffering, respect, and moral contempt play in Kant's responses to these anguished letters.

Maria von Herbert was the sister of Franz Paul von Herbert, a member of the industrial nobility of Klagenfurt, the patron of a white lead factory, and host of an intellectual anti-monarchist circle close to Friedrich Schiller. She reached out to Kant, whose authority she worshipped as if he were a kind of God, for guidance in regaining a reason to live following a failed relationship. Von Herbert addresses Kant seeking the solace she has not found in his writings following the rupture of her relationship, which dissolved as a result of a 'protracted lie' regarding the existence of a previous lover who seduced her into forfeiting her feminine honour. Most likely, the former love affair Maria mentions in her first letter to Kant resulted in a son born out of wedlock (Ritter 2021: 138–143), massively disrupting the life of von Herbert, as we will see in the next subsection. In these desperate circumstances, which bring to mind Jane Austen novels[61], von Herbert implores Kant for practical advice on how to regain her lost attachment to life:

> Oh my heart splits into a thousand pieces, if I hadn't read so much of your work I would certainly have taken my own life by now, but the conclusion I had to draw from your theory stops me – it is wrong for me to die because my life is tormented, and I am instead supposed to live because of my being, now put yourself in my place and either damn me or give me solace, ... answer me, I implore you, or you yourself can't act according to your own imperative (Letter from Maria von Herbert 1791, Corr 11: 274).

Given Kant's aseptic attitude towards human emotions, his response to the young woman's request, which he deemed excessive, is revealing. Prima facie he attempts to act as a 'moral physician' would do, not as a 'flatterer', conveying to von Herbert that she must pay attention to the usual parts of a religious sermon, that is, *doctrine* [*Lehre*] and *discipline* [*Strafe*], which together provide the desired *solace* [*Trost*][62], once the deranged mind recovers from its previous

---

advancement of women, especially intellectual, imaginative women, an ambivalence surprising in a philosopher renowned for championing universal 'respect for persons.'

[61] As Garrath Williams reminds me, Austen avoids melodrama. In this vein, a novel such as *Northanger Abbey* satirizes gothic novels for indulging in this depiction of women as fragile and fickle beings.

[62] Taking solace into account, Kant does not lose the hope that the spiteful lover of Maria von Herbert will forgive her, at least if the love born between them is more moral than physical. See Corr 11: 334: 'When your change in attitude has been revealed to your beloved friend —and the sincerity of your words makes it impossible to mistake this— only time will be needed to quench little by little the traces of his indignation (a justified feeling and one that is even based on the concepts of virtue) and to transform his indifference into a more firmly grounded love. If this should fail to happen, the earlier warmth of his affection was more physical than moral and, in view of the transient nature of such a love, would have vanished in time all by itself.'

discomfort (Letter to Maria von Herbert 1792, Corr 11: 334). The philosopher promulgates a doctrine regarding the importance of distinguishing *reticence* from *lack of sincerity* in practical behaviour: as the former acts from the fear 'that to reveal himself completely would make him despised by others', the latter displays falseness in the utterance of thoughts. In this way, reticence results from the finitude of human nature, and does not spoil character, while dishonesty corrupts thinking as a positive evil, given that the dishonest speaker is aware of the falsehood of his speech. According to Kant, the former relationship of Maria von Herbert has not been merely concealed, as the woman positively lied about her lover, a transgression which 'subverts the dignity of man in our own person and attacks the root of our thinking'. (Letter to Maria von Herbert 1792, Corr 11: 332). Thus, Kant sides with the beloved man to whom von Herbert gave all of her love, and who lost his trust in her and his love for her after the young woman demonstrated herself incapable of virtue. When considering Kant's merciless reaction to the clear emptiness and desperation that Maria von Herbert was experiencing, a key element of the correspondence is Kant's rebuke for having lied to her former lover, having concealed the existence of a previous one. When considering the strict morals women had to respect in Kant's time, her decision might also be considered not 'a disclosure of [a] lie' (Corr 11: 333), but rather a brave act of *parrhesia*, which few women would have dared perform in a highly patriarchal society. Kant, however, is adamant that von Herbert's fault lies in the mendacity of her confession regarding her previous lover, as, given that she was a woman, she was expected not to have had any previous romantic experiences.[63] In this case, Kant fails to appreciate that moral laws are often intertwined with social *mores*, which have a greater impact on women than men, as women must protect their supposed sexual honour. Thus, Kant decides to respond to the request of Maria von Herbert with a formal and neutral interpretation of honesty as moral virtue, without acknowledging the potential moral value of the confession about her previous lover. He also reminds her that life includes misfortunes which must be faced with composure. While Kant's counsel to behave with reticence might result in more hypocrisy than virtue, yet he neglects to mention this in his evaluation of the case.[64]

It is also noteworthy that after replying to von Herbert, Kant asked a mutual acquaintance, J. B. Erhard, how she had reacted to his letter. Erhard answered

---

[63] Varden (2020a: 161–162) delivers an accurate account of the distance between lying and reticence that Kant's moral theory allows to cast light on the options of Maria von Herbert to prevent to lie to her new special friend about her previous intimate past.

[64] Ritter's account of Kant's reaction to von Herbert's first letter sets forth a more positive interpretation of the role of the philosopher as a 'moral physician.' See Ritter (2021: 147–149).

that '[Maria von Herbert] has capsized on the reef of romantic love. In order to realize an idealistic love, she gave herself to a man who misused her trust. And then, trying to achieve such love with another, she told her new lover about the previous one' (Corr 11: 407). While he also adds that 'I think she could still be saved' (Corr 11: 407) if she would have a little more *délicatesse,* Erhard states that 'hypersensitivity, private delusions, and fantasies' have spoiled von Herbert's moral judgement and imagination, leading to regrettable consequences.

After the first letter, Maria von Herbert continued to send others to Kant, who seems to have left them unanswered. In her second letter, the woman states that 'the commandments of morality are too trifling for me' (Letter from Maria von Herbert 1793, Corr 11: 401) and asks Kant for advice in putting an end to the 'unbearable emptiness of soul' she is suffering from. She also states her intention to visit the professor in Königsberg so as to hear Kant's 'life story' and what had dissuaded him from marrying and having a family. It is easy to imagine the annoyance that such a proposal might have caused in Kant, a (somewhat misogynistic) confirmed bachelor. Maria von Herbert further describes herself as seized by a state of apathy impeding her from experiencing any pleasure in life and human interaction, and even leading her to contemplate suicide. While Kant ceased replying to this uncomfortable correspondence, he did forward von Herbert's subsequent letters to the wife of an English salesman, Elisabeth Motherby[65], known to be a honourable and virtuous woman. Kant seems to have sent these letters as a sort of warning to Motherby about the threats that 'curious' mental derangement could pose to women and their integration in society, especially as Motherby and her husband were raising a daughter. Most likely, Kant had drawn the conclusion that von Herbert's malaise was the result of a simple mental disorder, which he considered could be solved through the application of mental effort and moral willingness to combat the nihilism so common in the human mind.

In her third letter, Marie von Herbert shares with Kant that Erhard told her that Kant had inquired about her, begging him for more moral guidance, as she feels that Kant understands better than anyone the influence his writings have had on her life. Von Herbert describes the extreme suffering she is experiencing, and continually grapples with which course of direction to follow. She also

---

[65] See the Letter to Elisabeth Motherby 1793, Corr 11: 411–412: 'A number of expressions, especially in the first letter, refer to writings of mine that she read and are difficult to understand without an explanation. You have been so fortunate in the upbringing you have received that I do not need to commend these letters to you as an example of warning, to guard you against the aberrations of a sublimated fantasy. Nevertheless they may serve to make your perception of that good fortune all the more lively.' See Langton (1992: 497, 499).

depicts her psychic suffering as turmoil resulting from antinomies, which only her decision to commit suicide helps to overcome:

> Since I assume that you are interested in the fate of anyone who owes as much to your guidance as I do, I want to tell you of my spiritual progress and my frame of mind. . . . . . . I think that death, from an egoistic point of view, must be the most pleasant thing for every true human being, and only if people take morality and friends into account can they with the greatest desire to die still wish for life and try to preserve it no matter what (Letter from Maria von Herbert 1794, Corr 11: 485–486).

While the suffering Maria von Herbert expresses in her letters seems to concern the wise professor of Königsberg, it does not move him to a compassionate attitude towards the young woman, as he also left her third letter unanswered. Von Herbert committed suicide nine years later, drowning herself in the Drau River after a family party. Eight years later, in 1811, her brother Baron Franz Paul would also commit suicide. This failed correspondence between Kant and an anguished von Herbert highlights certain interesting material conditions playing a role in the respect for human dignity. I suggest two final remarks about Kant's strict judgement of this woman's despair. First, Kant's appraisal of von Herbert's behaviour insists on the moral requirement of enduring pain, labour, and suffering, which, notably, Kant does not ascribe to the *animus effeminatus*, understood as 'the inability to endure evils' (Eth-Vigil § 103, 27: 645). Instead, Kant mentions *patience*, the 'ability to get used to suffering hardships' (Eth-Vigil §103, 27: 645), (also traditionally a more feminine than masculine trait) as a helpful psychological tool for resisting evils and misfortune. Second, Kant conjectures in the *Anthropology from a Pragmatic Point of View* that suicide committed by individuals suffering from mental disorders is an example of cowardice – not courage – as the subject is unable in such cases to find the inner strength of will necessary for coping with the disappointments of life:

> It seems to be a kind of heroism to the human being to look death straight in the eye and not fear it, when he can no longer love life. But if, although he fears death, he still cannot stop loving life in all circumstances, so that in order to proceed to suicide a mental disorder stemming from anguish must precede, then he dies of cowardice, because he can no longer bear the agonies of life (Anth § 77, 7: 258).

According to these anthropological remarks regarding the cultural history of suicide, Kant states that those constantly complaining about the miserable lives they must endure ultimately seek to conflate two desires into one, that is, the desire to live a long life, and the desire to feel happiness and satisfaction. Kant's moral theory, however, seeks to foster a character able to manage all possible setbacks and difficulties. In this way, the lack of a response to Maria von Herbert seems to relate to the fact that she did not intend to reclaim her own will, but rather approached Kant attempting to use philosophy as a means to self-fulfilment. On the contrary, the human doer must be aware of the weaknesses ensuing from her finitude, and consequently exercise patience in accepting the setbacks of life with calm and composure.[66] Such obstacles, in Kant's view, are not seen as valid reasons for losing one's will to live.

5.2 The Sense of Honour as a Source of Female Suffering: Kant's Legal Plea for Unmarried Mothers

Kant focuses on the infanticides perpetrated by single mothers in a section of the *Doctrine of Right* (DR 6: 335–337) shedding light on certain consequences ensuing from the nature of the civil union. In his view, the situation of these women represents a quandary for penal justice, as 'the public justice arising from the state becomes an *injustice* from the perspective of the justice arising from the people' (DR 6: 337) The dilemma consists in the fact that the judge cannot take the concept of honour denied to unwed women as an illusion, but rather as a moral condition that all women should meet under threat of exclusion from society and ignominy.[67] Given this situation, it is not completely fair that penal justice condemns the infanticide committed. Moreover, penal justice is a balance between the suspicion of cruelty and indulgency, at least until a 'barbarous and underdeveloped' (DR 6: 337) legislation is modified to consider the difficult situation facing women in such circumstances.[68]

My aim in this subsection will be to determine whether, in the course of his enquiry, Kant recognizes the entangled situation of single mothers resulting from the competing social pressures of motherhood and feminine honour. In my view, Kant succeeds in highlighting a social structure mired in injustice that will not be remedied until legislation ceases to sanction the torture, beat, or publicly

---

[66] See Kant's remarks about the detrimental influence of mental illness on bodily and mental health, related to the 'art of prolonging human life' claimed by Professor Hufeland. See CF 7: 99: 'Take a sick person who has been lying for years in a hospital bed, suffering and indigent, and hear how often he wishes that death would come soon and deliver him from his misery. Do not believe him: He is not in earnest about it. Though his reason does prompt him to wish for death, his natural instinct is to live.'

[67] Kant's *Lectures on Anthropology* hint to the special attention that the husband must devote to the chastity of his wife. See Anth-Fried 25: 714: 'the man demands the same abstinence of his wife in marriage as before marriage, and is very jealous in this'. Kant claims that the marriage opens an emancipatory horizon for the woman, while for the man means a threshold of several sacrifices and renounces to his former freedom.

[68] In this excerpt, Kant also references the duel as a socially motivated masculine habit analogous to the protection of women's honour, which in turn affects the social construction of masculine subjectivity. In fact, as was common in the eighteenth century, men were expected to settle disagreements through public fights.

demean vulnerable women. Various Kantian scholars have offered different interpretations of these passages from the *Doctrine of Right*. Timmermann claims that 'Kant is not ... advocating lenience but certain legislative reforms, which are needed to dispel the perception that capital punishment is unjust' (Timmermann 2022: 1). This interpreter dissects the discussion about maternal infanticide in a) a standard view that discards capital punishment for the mother as the newborn is considered illegitimate; b) a reading that allows punishment as sexual mores change and the child is recognized by the law; and c) an interpretation that rejects the child's murder under any circumstance. Taking this interpretation into account, I will engage in a dialogue with sundry interpreters seeking to grasp the aims of Kant's apparent defence of unwed women (Wood 1999: 370, f.31; Sussman 2008: 33; Pascoe 2011: 5; Mertens 2017: 461). The following passage from the *Doctrine of Right* analyses the thorny issue of illegitimate children:

> A child that comes into the world apart from marriage is born outside the law (for the law is marriage) and therefore outside the protection of the law. It has, as it were, stolen into the commonwealth (like contraband merchandise), so that the commonwealth can ignore its existence (since it was not right that it should have come to exist in this way), and can therefore also ignore its annihilation; and no decree can remove the mother's shame when it becomes known that she gave birth without being married (DR 6: 336).

In this account, Kant highlights the impact of shame on the decision to murder a newborn who will not be recognized by the commonwealth.[69] Kant suggests that civil society will guarantee the survival of these children rejected due to their illegitimate origin in sexual intercourse before marriage. Timmermann (2022: 13) claims that Kant does not truly view the newborn out of wedlock as 'contraband' inserted illegally within the commonwealth, but rather that he describes a view of natural children common among intellectuals of his time. Cesare Beccaria, highly criticized by Kant in the section of the *Doctrine of Right* regarding capital punishment, argues in his well-known writing *Dei delitti e delle pene* that to forfeit one's honour would entail the subject's regression to the state of nature (Beccaria 1766: 47). Since the middle ages, torture, physical punishment, and execution were common in the German legislation on both maternal infanticide and sexual intercourse before marriage.[70] While Kant does not see capital punishment as an instrument that degrades human dignity in the case of homicides (DR 6: 463), but rather as the result of a fully

---

[69] This desperate action would be immortalized in German literature a decade later through the character of Margarete in Goethe's *Faust*.

[70] See a complete historical overview of the legal framework of unwed women in Timmermann (2022: 22–23).

realized system of public justice, he considers that religious penance demeans the human dignity of unwed mothers. This is a key element for better grasping his remarks regarding the situation of unwed women committing infanticide.

In my view, Kant does not argue for leniency in the case of infanticide committed by unwed mothers as an exception to the ruling function of penal justice regarding the enforcement of sexual mores. Thus, I fully concur with Timmermann in claiming that Kant does not regard capital punishment as the fairest legal decision against the homicide that infanticide entails. Instead, he recommends that institutions and foundling homes protect children begotten outside of wedlock.[71] As in the case of poverty relief, Kant references 'elderly unmarried people of both sexes' (DR 6: 326) as a key element in finding a solution to the abandonment and murder of illegitimate newborns, as '[elderly unmarried people] are in part to blame for there being abandoned children' (DR 6: 326). This last remark clearly places some of the responsibility for these children born out of wedlock on male 'confirmed bachelors', who the passage addresses as the likely culprits of the seduction and consequent social vilification of unwed women. In any case, Kant hesitates to advance his own proposals, which he deems quite tentative, as he is aware of the difficulties of solving this problem without offending either the rule of law or morality (DR 6: 327). In this same vein, in another section regarding the rights ensuing from the nature of the civil union, Kant sets forward measures such as the following:

> As for maintaining those children abandoned because of poverty or shame, or indeed murdered because of this, the state has a right to charge the people with the duty of not knowingly letting them die, even though they are an unwelcome addition to the population (DR 6: 326).

The recourse to unmarried bachelors of both sexes, (which likely included widowers who did not remarry) to guarantee the maintenance of illegitimate children represents a demand that the wealthy segment of the commonwealth subsidizes its most vulnerable members. Importantly, men and women are affected by different obstacles resulting from the loss of their honour. While men must cope with the label of cowardice, women face social ignominy. It is also important to highlight that in the quoted passage Kant considers newborns

---

[71] Pascoe (2019) sets forth an interesting interpretation of Kant's account of infanticide committed by unmarried women by understanding their distressing situation as a return to the 'state of nature', where the foetus would have only provisional rights, depending on the 'innate right' of the mother. Moving from a key passage of DV 6: 336–337, Pascoe draws a conclusion which I fully agree with (Pascoe 2019: 23–24): 'The implication of Kant's argument is that, were the state just, the conditions that create infanticide would no longer exist, and the law could punish it as murder. I cannot go as far as Kant here. ... But Kant's insight is nevertheless essential to the contemporary debate about reproductive rights: abortion is not a problem to be solved by restrictive legislation but by broad social and legislative change.'

born out of wedlock 'an unwelcome addition to the population', which supports the argument that he views these births as 'contraband' smuggled into the commonwealth. This civil reformist agenda thus seeks to remedy the injustice stoked by the combination of barbaric religious punishments, penal justice, and morality common in Kant's time. We cannot however, affirm, without incurring in overstatement, that Kant's argument is motivated by his solidarity with the unfortunate fate of unmarried mothers. As we have seen before, emotions, in Kant's view, should never guide the practical reflection.[72] That said, these pages of the *Doctrine of Right*, clearly confirm his commitment to the improvement of the German institutions managing such moral quandaries, following action taken by the monarch Frederick the Great, who implemented 'bio-political' measures to detect clandestine pregnancies in Prussia and thus avoid eventual murders of newborns.[73]

The actions of the public authority regarding crimes related to female honour are intertwined, to some extent, with a history of 'bio-politics', as the vulnerabilities and strengths of the population are intended to offset the shortcomings of excluded social groups. Once again, Kant does not provide an account of social suffering based on the direct experience of unmarried mothers. That said, his view of the commonwealth still promotes providing support to those unfortunate individuals who have fallen into social dishonour, appealing to their inalienable human dignity, as in the case of poverty. Moreover, Kant seems to focus on the fact that infanticide of children born out of wedlock could be avoided if due measures were taken, which would also free these women from the oppression of religious authorities. Here, then, he manifests some awareness of the fact that the commonwealth should not ostracize dishonoured women, but on the contrary, provide them support in grappling with the threat of social ignominy through a regulated cooperation of individuals (taxation of bachelors of both sexes) – and the public authority (the foundation of foundling institutions run by the state). In sum, the Kantian commonwealth is quite sensitive to the barbaric spectacle of women suffering social condemnation, and does promote a determined agenda to progressively reduce the tensions between morality and right. In Kant's view, individual agents are to be charged with a social responsibility that the public authority embodied in the lawgiver must also secure.[74]

---

[72] See on this point Uleman (2000).
[73] On this issue see Timmermann (2022: 25, f.60) and Hull (1996: 111–113).
[74] About the institutional making of civil personhood in Kant see Pascoe (2011: 25): 'Personhood is institutionally constructed. . . . [Rights and protection] are extended through institutions that turn on public recognition and consent.' In my view, Kant also allocates some puzzling responsibility to individual action in the making of social identity, which is partly encouraged to remedy social crises which the institutional agency is unable to manage, as mentioned in subsection 4.2.

6 Conclusions

This essay has addressed Kant's elusive account of social suffering, requiring the interpreter to read between the lines of Kant's texts to provide an overview of the way his practical philosophy accounts for the failures resulting from the exclusion from political membership, the frustrations of misfortune, and the ignominy stemming from the transgression of sexual mores. Kant does not ignore the experience of social suffering. Nonetheless, neither does he undertake a complete survey of the social and political structures and agendas hindering moral and civil human development. None of the aforementioned social failures relinquishes the agency of the subject who undergoes them. Even unwed mothers do not seem to act from their own volition in violating moral impositions, but rather often from fraud, as their lovers may have promised them marriage, or as a result of domination and violence, in the case of rape and sexual exploitation. This account attempted to present social suffering as a thorny issue for Kant's ideals of both autonomy and the political commonwealth, insofar as the positive contribution of well off citizens is required to relieve indigence or social condemnation understood as a woeful stage of human abuse and injustice.

Kant's support for relieving passive segments of the commonwealth from their exclusion from any productive role or from 'civil death' tends towards the image of the virtuous subject as a strong, robust subject, accustomed to resisting unmoved against twists of fate. In this way, the support of the state is regarded as a provisional measure that should not spoil the capacity of the individual subject to 'work his way up' (DR § 46, 6: 315) in an allegedly meritocratic market. Furthermore, the ideal of the moral subject urges fostering a resilient faculty of desire, not easily captivated by vain whims, but rather resolved to comply with universal maxims, reducing the effects of injustice and abuse in society. Kant's demands on individual subjects do not address the often detrimental effects that social status, gender, or race might have on their advancement within society,[75] struggling to detect situations of intolerable oppression and domination. Given this, Kant's contemporary interpreters are faced with a promising research horizon[76], in studying how domination may underpin social interaction

---

[75] In Kant's view, social agency does not take into account any structural disadvantage hindering the promotion of the social agent. On the contrary, the higher faculty of desire should overcome manifold burdens through a sheer determination of character, which makes it difficult to engage in any fruitful dialogue with theorists of reification and oppression (see Shklar 1990; Young 2011; Renault 2017).

[76] Pascoe has neatly formulated this challenge. See Pascoe (2022: 53): 'Kant's account of justice is famously systemic, developing an institutional account of the state designed to support freedom and prevent domination. But Kant's accounts of domination and oppression are pointedly *not* systemic, relying either on his anthropological arguments about gender and his theory of race, or

among alleged equals. A positive interpretation of Kant's account of the commonwealth, however, draws on ideas such as the commitment to rewarding animals for their service to human beings, and the suggestion not to demean the inalienable humanity of mentally disordered persons. Moreover, Kant's account of poverty relief illustrates his view that poor people are not animals, and, in consequence, they must be treated with the respect appropriate to the humanity they too embody.[77]

It is a matter of fact that Kant's moral pedagogy, emphasizing the effort the subject must make to meet the conditions of human dignity, tends to diminish the existence of structural flaws in the commonwealth, insofar as public injustices are often concealed given their understanding as the result of personal failures. In this vein, Kant recommends people give meaning to their lives through action, resisting the inclination to take a merely passive attitude towards life. Such a moral framework reflects a narrow account of the social tragedy of poverty, as well as of suffering resulting from the social condemnation of unwed mothers, insofar as the original causes leading to such sad outcomes are not directly addressed. The state merely requests wealthy citizens provide assistance to their vulnerable fellow members, without providing any solutions for these to reclaim their social agency. In practice, however, many levels of precarity must be combatted before attempting to control an epidemic of poverty or maternal infanticide. In both cases, welfare as a universal right, and protection against sexual domination should be analysed as inalienable material features of a systematic theory of justice. The increasing global ideological tendency to view social suffering as the result of personal failures tends to obscure this social pathology, just as it occurred in Kant's time. This requires us to be more attentive to the rhythm of social progress and regression, and the contribution that the history of philosophy might provide in expanding civil rights and eradicating suffering ingrained in social structures.

Progressive political theory must take on the challenge of reimagining our societies, reconsidering the value we ascribe to the suffering of others and our own responsibility for it. While Kant's ideal of autonomy neglects suffering caused by social structures, seeing it as an individual burden, some of Kant's

---

on claims about individual immaturity . . .. This gap informs contemporary claims that Kant's theory of justice can be reconstructed or rescued from concerns about raced or gendered oppression, since it does not *structurally* embed this oppression, relying on it only empirically, historically, or circumstantially.'

[77] In footnote 31, I outline why my Element does not focus on the suffering stemming from chattel slavery. In my view, this source of injustice should be tackled in an account of Kant's theory of international political order, as Kant's late criticism of colonialism (Kleingeld 2014) does not chiefly address the suffering of racialized slaves nor a hypothetical response to it by individual states, but rather rebukes the complicity of the states in plural in such a breach of the international law, which must be eradicated from the earth.

writings might inspire us to rephrase the mitigation of social suffering as a civil commitment for the state and the citizenry as a whole. Kant does not develop a full-fledged theory regarding social vulnerability, exclusion, oppression, and domination, nor does he understand the causes of these phenomena as problems that a public political agenda ought to amend. This, however, presents new horizons for scholars: the challenge of reformulating aspects of his thought to render them fully consistent with the a priori grounds of his account of human dignity and the development of the human civil commonwealth seems to be a promising task.

Abbreviations of Kant's Works

Anth *Anthropologie in pragmatischer Hinsicht / Anthropology from a pragmatic point of view* [in *Anthropology, History and Education*, pp. 227–429] AA 7

Corr *Briefe / Correspondence* AA 11

Anth-Fried *Vorlesungen Wintersemester 1775/1776 Friedländer / Anthropology Friedländer 1775/76* [In *Lectures on Anthropology*, pp. 43–256] AA 25

Anth-Mensch *Vorlesungen Wintersemester 1781/1782 Menschenkunde / Anthropology Menschenkunde 1781/82* [In *Lectures on Anthropology*, pp. 281–333] AA 25

Anth-Mron *Vorlesungen Wintersemester 1784/1785 Mrongovius / Anthropology Mrongovius 1784/85* [In *Lectures on Anthropology*, pp. 339–510] AA 25

CB *Mutmasslicher Anfang der Menschengeschichte / Conjectural Beginning of Human History* [in *Anthropology, History and Education*, pp. 160–175] AA 8

CF *Der Streit der Fakultäten / The Conflict of the Faculties* [in *Religion and Rational Theology*, pp. 233–328] AA 7

CJ *Kritik der Urteilskraft / Critique of the Power of Judgment* AA 5

Refl *Reflexionen / Reflections* AA 14–19

DR/DV *Rechtslehre – Tugendlehre / Doctrine of Right – Doctrine of Virtue* [in *Practical Philosophy*, pp. 353–604] AA 6

Eth-Collins *Vorlesungen Wintersemester 1772/1773 Collins / Moral Philosophy: From the Lectures of Professor Kant. Taken by Georg Ludwig Collins 1772/73* [In *Lectures on Ethics*, pp. 37–222]. AA 27

Eth-Vigil *Vorlesungen Wintersemester 1793/1794 Die Metaphysik der Sitten Vigilantius / Notes on the Lectures of Mr. Kant on the Metaphysics of Morals* [In *Lectures on Ethics*, pp. 249–452]. AA 27

Eth(PP)-Herder *Praktische Philosophie Herder / Practical Philosophy Herder* (1763/64 or 64/65) [In *Lectures on Ethics*, pp. 1–36]. AA 27

FS *Die falsche Spitzfindigkeit der vier syllogistischen Figuren erwiesen / The False Sublety of the Four Syllogistic Figures* [In *Theoretical Philosophy* 1755–1770, pp. 85–106] AA 2

G *Grundlegung zur Metaphysik der Sitten / Groundwork of the Metaphysics of Morals* [in *Practical Philosophy*, pp. 37–108] AA 4

IUH *Idee zu einer allgemeiner Geschichte in weltbürgerlicher Absicht / Idea for a Universal History with a Cosmopolitan Aim* [in *Anthropology, History and Education*, pp. 107–120] AA 8

KPrR *Kritik der praktischen Vernunft / Critique of Practical Reason* [in *Practical Philosophy*, pp. 133–272] AA 5

L-NR *Naturrecht Feyerabend (Winter 1784) / Natural Right Course Notes by Feyerabend* [in *Lectures and Drafts on Political Philosophy*, pp. 73–1394] AA 27

MH *Versuch über die Krankheiten des Kopfes / Essay on the Maladies of the Head* [in *Anthropology, History and Education*, pp. 63–77] AA 02

OFBS *Beobachtungen über das Gefühl des Schönen und Erhabenen / Observations on the Feeling of the Beautiful and Sublime* [in *Anthropology, History and Education*, pp. 18–62] AA 2

PP *Zum ewigen Frieden / Toward Perpetual Peace* [in *Practical Philosophy*, pp. 311–352] AA 8

Rel *Die Religion innerhalb der Grenzen der bloßen Vernunft / Religion Within the Boundaries of Mere Reason* [in *Religion and Rational Theology*, pp. 39–216]. AA 6

WIE *Beantwortung der Frage: Was ist Aufklärung? / An Answer to the Question: What is Enlightenment* [in *Practical Philosophy*, pp. 11–22] AA 8

Bibliography

Adorno, Theodor Wiesengrund (1973) [1966]. *Negative Dialectics*. Translated by E. B. Ashton, London: Routledge.

Allais, Lucy (2014). 'What Properly Belongs to Me: Kant on Giving to Beggars'. *Journal of Moral Philosophy* 12(6): 754–771.

Baiasu, Sorin (2014). 'Kant's Justification of Welfare'. *Diametros* 39: 1–28.

Baron, Marcia (1995). *Kantian Ethics Almost without Apology*. Ithaca: Cornell University Press.

Baron, Marcia and Fahmy, Melissa (2009). 'Beneficence and Other Duties of Love in *The Metaphysics of Morals*'. In *Kant's Ethics*, edited by Thomas E. Hill, pp. 209–228, Oxford: Blackwell.

Beccaria, Cesare (1766). *Dei delitti e delle pene*. Harlem. Published anonymously. 5th ed.

Blöser, Claudia (2023). 'Global Poverty and Kantian Hope'. *Ethical Theory and Moral Practice* 26: 287–302.

Cholbi, Michael (2000). 'Kant and the Irrationality of Suicide'. *History of Philosophy Quarterly* 17(2): 159–176.

Cicero, Marcus Tullius (1913). *De Officiis*. Translation by Walter Miller. Cambridge, MA: Harvard University Press.

Davies, Luke (2023). 'Kant on Civil Self-Sufficiency'. *Archiv für Geschichte der Philosophie* 105(1): 118–140.

Davies, Luke (2020). 'Kant on Welfare: 5 Unsuccessful Defences'. *Kantian Review* 25(1): 1–25.

Denis, Lara (2000). 'Kant's Conception of Duties Regarding Animals: Reconstruction and Reconsideration'. *History of Philosophy Quarterly* 17: 405–423.

Formosa, Paul and Sticker, Martin (2019). 'Kant and the Demandingness of the Virtue of Beneficence'. *European Journal of Philosophy* 27: 625–642.

Fricker, Miranda (2007). *Epistemic Injustice: Power & the Ethics of Knowing*. Oxford: Oxford University Press.

Gilabert, Pablo (2010). 'Kant and the Claims of the Poor'. *Philosophy and Phenomenological Research* 81(2): 382–418.

González, Ana Marta (2020). *Kant on Culture, Happiness and Civilization*. Cham: Palgrave McMillan.

Hasan, Rafeeq (2018). 'Freedom and Poverty in the Kantian State'. *European Journal of Philosophy* 26: 911–931.

Hatfield, Elaine, Cacioppo, John T., and Rapson, Richard L. (1993). 'Emotional Contagion'. *Current Directions in Psychological Science* 2(3): 96–99.

Hay, Carol (2020). 'What Do We Owe to Animals? Kant on Non-Intrinsic Value'. In *Kant and Animals*, edited by Lucy Allais and John Callanan, pp. 176–190. Oxford: Oxford University Press.

Hegel, Georg Wilhelm Friedrich. (1821/2003). *Elements of the Philosophy of Right* (cited as GPhR). Edited by Allen Wood and translated by H. B. Nisbet. Cambridge: Cambridge University Press.

Holtman, Sarah (2018). *Kant on Civil Society and Welfare*. Cambridge: Cambridge University Press.

Hull, Isabel (1996). *Sexuality, State, and Civil Society in Germany (1700–1815)*. Ithaca, NY: Cornell University Press.

Kain, Patrick (2010). 'Duties Regarding Animals'. In *Kant's Metaphysics of Morals: A Critical Guide*, edited by Lara Denis, pp. 210–233. Cambridge: Cambridge University Press.

Kant, I. (1992). *Theoretical Philosophy 1755–1770*. Edited and translated by David Walford and Ralf Meerbote. Cambridge: Cambridge University Press.

Kant, I. (1996). *The Metaphysics of Morals*. Edited and translated by Mary Gregor. Cambridge: Cambridge University Press.

Kant, I. (1996a). *Religion and Rational Theology*. Edited and translated by Allen W. Wood and George di Giovanni. Cambridge: Cambridge University Press.

Kant, I. (1996b). *Practical Philosophy*. Edited and translated by Mary J. Gregor. Cambridge: Cambridge University Press.

Kant, I. (1997). *Lectures on Ethics*. Edited by Peter Heath and J. B. Schneewind. Cambridge: Cambridge University Press.

Kant, I. (1999). *Correspondence*. Edited and translated by Arnulf Zweig. Cambridge: Cambridge University Press.

Kant, I. (2007). *Anthropology, History and Education*. Edited by Günter Zöller and Robert Louden. Cambridge: Cambridge University Press.

Kant, I. (2012). *Lectures on Anthropology*. Edited and translated by Allen W. Wood, Robert Louden, Robert Clewis, and Felicitas Munzel. Cambridge: Cambridge University Press.

Kant, I. (2016). *Lectures and Drafts on Political Philosophy*. Edited and translated by Frederick Rauscher.

Katrin, Flikschuh (2010). 'Justice without Virtue'. In *Kant's Metaphysics of Morals: A Critical Guide*, edited by Lara Denis, pp. 51–70. Cambridge: Cambridge University Press.

Kleingeld, Pauline (2014). 'Kant's Second Thoughts on Colonialism'. In *Kant and Colonialism: Historical and Critical Perspectives*, edited by Katrin Flikschuh and Lea Ypi, pp. 43–67. Oxford: Oxford University Press.

Kleinman, Arthur, Veena, Das, and Margaret, Lock (ed.) (1997). *Social Suffering*. Berkeley: University of California Press.

Korsgaard, Christine (2018). *Fellow Creatures: Our Obligations to the Other Animals*. New York: Oxford University Press.

Langton, Rae (1992). 'Duty and Desolation'. *Philosophy* 67(262): 481–505.

Levine, Stephen K. (2009). *Trauma, Tragedy, Therapy: The Arts and Human Suffering*. London: Jessica Kingsley.

Loriaux, Sylvie (2023). 'Kant on Social Justice: Poverty, Dependence, and Depersonification'. *The Southern Journal of Philosophy* 61(1): 233–256.

Loriaux, Sylvie (2020). *Kant and Global Distributive Justice*. Cambridge: Cambridge University Press.

Lu-Adler, Huaping (2022). 'Kant and Slavery – Or Why He Never Became a Racial Egalitarian'. *Critical Philosophy of Race* 10(2): 263–294.

Lucretius (1951). *De Rerum Natura*. Translated by Ronald Latham. Harmondsworth: Penguin Books.

Mahon, James Edwin (2006). 'Kant and Maria Von Herbert: Reticence vs. Deception'. *Philosophy* 81(317): 417–444.

Malpas, Jeff and Lickiss, Norelle. (2012). *Perspectives on Human Suffering*. Edited by Jeff Malpas and Norelle Lickiss. New York: Springer.

Meier, Georg Friedrich (1749). *Versuch eines neuen Lehrgebäudes von den Seelen der Thiere*. Halle: Verlegts Carl Herrmann Hemmerde.

Mertens, Thomas (2017). 'Emergencies and Criminal Law in Kant's Legal Philosophy'. *ethic@* 16: 459–474.

Michaelis, Christian Friedrich (1785–1786). 'Tollheit aus Mitleidenschaft', in *Medicinisch-Praktische Bibliothek*. Göttingen: Bey Johann Christian Dieterich.

Mieth, Corinna and Williams, Garrath (2022). 'Beyond (Non)-Instrumentalization: Migration and Dignity within a Kantian Framework'. *Ethical Theory and Moral Practice* 26(2): 209–224.

Mieth, Corinna and Williams, Garrath (2021). 'Poverty, Dignity, and the Kingdom of Ends'. In *Human Dignity and the Kingdom of Ends: Kantian Perspectives and Practical Applications*, edited by Jan-Willem van der Rijt and Adam Steven Cureton, pp. 206–223. New York: Routledge.

Moran, Kate A. (2017). 'Neither Justice nor Charity? Kant on "General Injustice"'. *Canadian Journal of Philosophy* 47: 477–498.

Müller, Nico D. (2022). *Kantianism for Animals: A Radical Kantian Animal Ethic*. New York: Palgrave Macmillan.

O'Neill, Onora (1989). 'Universal Laws and End-in-themselves'. *The Monist* 72(3): 341–346.

Pascoe, Jordan (2022). *Kant's Theory of Labour*. Cambridge: Cambridge University Press.

Pascoe, Jordan (2019). 'On Finding Yourself in a State of Nature: A Kantian Account of Abortion and Voluntary Motherhood'. *Feminist Philosophy Quarterly* 5(3): 1–28.

Pascoe, Jordan (2011). 'Personhood, Protection, and Promiscuity: Kant on Infanticide and Institutions'. *APA Newsletter on Philosophy and Feminism* 10(2): 1–31.

Pinheiro Walla, Alice (2019). 'A Kantian Foundation for Welfare Rights'. *Jurisprudence* 1: 1–16.

Pinzani, Alessandro (2023). 'Towards a Kantian Argument for a Universal Basic Income'. *Ethical Theory and Moral Practice* 26: 225–235.

Pinzani, Alessandro and Sánchez Madrid, Nuria (2016). 'The State Looks Down: Some Reassessments of Kant's Appraisal of Citizenship'. In *Kant and Social Policies*, edited by Andrea Faggion, Nuria Sánchez Madrid, and Alessandro Pinzani, pp. 25–48. Cham: Palgrave Macmillan.

Pybus, Elizabeth, and Broadie, Alexander (1978). 'Kant and the Maltreatment of Animals'. *Philosophy* 53(206): 560–561.

Reimarus, Hermann Samuel (1762). *Allgemeine Betrachtungen über die Triebe der Thiere*. Hamburg: Bey Johann Carl Bohn.

Renault, Emmanuel (2017). *Social Suffering: Sociology, Psychology. Politics*. New York: Rowman & Littlefield.

Ripstein, Arthur (2009). *Force and Freedom: Kant's Legal and Political Philosophy*. Cambridge: Cambridge University Press.

Ritter, Bernhard (2021). 'Solace or Counsel for Death: Kant and Maria von Herbert'. In *Women and Philosophy in 18th Century Germany*, edited by Corey Dyck, pp. 137–156, Oxford: Oxford University Press.

Russel, Francey (2020). 'Kantian Self-Conceit and the Two Guises of Authority'. *Canadian Journal of Philosophy* 50(2): 268–283.

Salgueiro, Inês (2024). 'Kantian Animal Ethics, Deep Dignity, and the Moral Game'. *Environmental Philosophy* 21(1): 5–29.

Sánchez Madrid, Nuria (2025). 'Kant on Labor Relations: An Account of Economic Dependence from the Perspective of Non-ideal Social Philosophy'. *Philosophy of Social Sciences* 55 (4): 330–347.

Sánchez Madrid, Nuria (2023a). 'Kant on Social Suffering: Vulnerability as Moral and Legal Value'. In *Kant and the Problem of Politics*, edited by Luigi Caranti and Alessandro Pinzani, pp. 145–160, London: Routledge.

Sánchez Madrid, Nuria (2023b). 'Kant's Social Sympathy: Debunking Beneficence and Cultivating the Sense of Justice'. In *The Kantian Subject*, edited by Luigi Caranti and Fernando Silva, pp. 145–160, London: Routledge.

Sánchez Madrid, Nuria (2019). 'Poverty and Civil Recognition in Kant's Juridical Philosophy: Some Critical Remarks'. *Revista Portuguesa de Filosofia* 75: 565–582.

Sánchez Madrid, Nuria (2018). 'Kant on Poverty and Welfare: Social Demands and Juridical Goals in Kant's Doctrine of Right'. In *Kant's Doctrine of Right in the 21st Century*, edited by Larry Krasnoff, Paula Satne, and Nuria Sánchez Madrid, pp. 85–100. Cardiff: University of Wales Press.

Schaab, Janis David (2021). 'Kant and the Second Person'. *Journal of the American Philosophical Association* 7 (4): 494–513.

Sen, Amartya (2009). *The Idea of Justice*. Cambridge: Belknap.

Shklar, Judith (1990). *The Faces of Injustice*. New Haven: Yale University Press.

Sussman, David G. (2008). 'Shame and Punishment in Kant's "Doctrine of Right"'. *Philosophical Quarterly* 58: 299–317.

Svoboda, Toby (2015). *Duties Regarding Nature: A Kantian Environmental Ethic*. New York: Routledge.

Taraborrelli, Angela (2019). 'Cosmopolitanism and Space in Kant's Political Thought'. *Con-textos Kantianos: International Journal of Philosophy* 10: 15–26.

Timmermann, Jens (2022). 'The Quandary of Infanticide in Kant's "Doctrine of Right"'. *Archiv für Geschichte der Philosophie* 106(2): 1–28.

Timmermann, Jens (2016). 'Kant über Mitleidenschaft'. *Kant Studien* 107 (4):729–732.

Timmermann, Jens (2005). 'When the Tail Wags the Dog: Animal Welfare and Indirect Duty in Kantian Ethics'. *Kantian Review* 10: 128–149.

Uleman, Jennifer (2000). 'On Kant, Infanticide, and Finding Oneself on a State of Nature'. *Zeitschrift für philosophische Forschung* 54(2): 173–195.

Varden, Helga (2020a). *Sex, Love, and Gender: A Kantian Theory*. Oxford: Oxford University Press.

Varden, Helga (2020b). 'Kant and Moral Responsibility for Animals'. In *Kant and Animals*, edited by Lucy Allais and John J. Callanan, pp. 157–175. Oxford: Oxford University Press.

Varden, Helga (2015). 'Kant and Women'. *Pacific Philosophical Quarterly* 98(4): 1–42.

Vereb, Zachary (2021). 'Kant's Pre-critical Ontology and Environmental Philosophy'. *Environmental Philosophy* 18(1): 81–102.

Vilhauer, Benjamin (2024). *Kant on Rational Sympathy*. Cambridge: Cambridge University Press.

Vrousalis, Nicholas (2022). 'Interdependent Independence: Civil Self-Sufficiency and Productive Community in Kant's Theory of Citizenship'. *Kantian Review* 27(4): 443–460.

Wehofsits, Anna (2016). *Anthropologie und Moral: Affekte, Leidenschaft und Mitgefühl in Kants Ethik*. Berlin: Walter de Gruyter.

Weinrib, Ernest (2003). 'Poverty and Property in Kant's System of Rights'. *Notre Dame Law Review* 78: 795–828.

Wilkinson, Iain (2005). *Suffering: A Sociological Introduction* New York: Polity Press.

Wilson, Holly (2012). 'The Green Kant: Kant's Treatment of Animals'. In *Environmental Ethics: Readings in Theory and Application*, edited by Louis P. Pojman and Paul Pojman, pp. 62–70. Boston: Wadsworth.

Wood, Allen (1999). *Kant's Ethical Thought*. Cambridge: Cambridge University Press.

Young, Iris Marion (2011). *Responsibility for Justice*. Oxford: Oxford University Press.

Zweig, A. (1999). 'Introduction'. In I. Kant. *Correspondence*, edited by Arnulf Zweig, pp. 1–42, Cambridge: Cambridge University Press.

Acknowledgements

I especially wish to thank Howard Williams for having welcomed this Element as series editor of *Cambridge Elements. The Philosophy of Immanuel Kant*, and the anonymous editors of Cambridge University Press for their helpful remarks. I also wish to thank the Complutense Department of Philosophy and Society, and its director, Antonio Rivera, for making this Element possible by providing institutional support and funding for the proofreading of this text. I would like also to warmly thank Özlem Duva, Efraín Lazos, Pablo López Álvarez, Sylvie Loriaux, Jordan Pascoe, Garrath Williams, Angela Taraborrelli, and Helga Varden for their productive and supportive feedback on earlier drafts of this Element. Finally, I am especially indebted to Macarena Marey and Alice Pinheiro Walla for their inspiration as Kant scholars and for their engagement with my own research. Last but not least, I am thankful to Marshall Weiss for helping me with the copyediting of the last draft of this Element. This essay has been supported by the following funded research projects: the AEI Spanish research project *Labour Precarity, Body and Damaged Life. A Social Philosophy Research* (PID2019-105803GB-I0/AEI/10.13039/501100011033); the AEI Grant RED2022-134265-T, awarded by the MCIN/AEI/10.13039/501100011033, and the Cost Action CA20134 – *Traces as Research Agenda for Climate Change, Technology Studies, and Social Justice* (TRACTS).

Cambridge Elements

The Philosophy of Immanuel Kant

Desmond Hogan
Princeton University

Desmond Hogan joined the philosophy department at Princeton in 2004. His interests include Kant, Leibniz and German rationalism, early modern philosophy, and questions about causation and freedom. Recent work includes 'Kant on the Foreknowledge of Contingent Truths', *Res Philosophica* 91(1) (2014); 'Kant's Theory of Divine and Secondary Causation', in Brandon Look (ed.) *Leibniz and Kant*, Oxford University Press (2021); 'Kant and the Character of Mathematical Inference', in Carl Posy and Ofra Rechter (eds.) *Kant's Philosophy of Mathematics Vol. I*, Cambridge University Press (2020).

Howard Williams
University of Cardiff

Howard Williams was appointed Honorary Distinguished Professor at the Department of Politics and International Relations, University of Cardiff in 2014. He is also Emeritus Professor in Political Theory at the Department of International Politics, Aberystwyth University, a member of the Coleg Cymraeg Cenedlaethol (Welsh-language national college) and a Fellow of the Learned Society of Wales. He is the author of *Marx* (1980); *Kant's Political Philosophy* (1983); *Concepts of Ideology* (1988); *Hegel, Heraclitus and Marx's Dialectic* (1989); *International Relations in Political Theory* (1992); *International Relations and the Limits of Political Theory* (1996); *Kant's Critique of Hobbes: Sovereignty and Cosmopolitanism* (2003); *Kant and the End of War* (2012) and is currently editor of the journal Kantian Review. He is writing a book on the Kantian legacy in political philosophy for a new series edited by Paul Guyer.

Allen Wood
Indiana University

Allen Wood is Ward W. and Priscilla B. Woods Professor Emeritus at Stanford University. He was a John S. Guggenheim Fellow at the Free University in Berlin, a National Endowment for the Humanities Fellow at the University of Bonn and Isaiah Berlin Visiting Professor at the University of Oxford. He is on the editorial board of eight philosophy journals, five book series and The Stanford Encyclopedia of Philosophy. Along with Paul Guyer, Professor Wood is co-editor of The Cambridge Edition of the Works of Immanuel Kant and translator of the Critique of Pure Reason. He is the author or editor of a number of other works, mainly on Kant, Hegel and Karl Marx. His most recently published books are *Fichte's Ethical Thought*, Oxford University Press (2016) and *Kant and Religion*, Cambridge University Press (2020). Wood is a member of the American Academy of Arts and Sciences.

About the Series

This Cambridge Elements series provides an extensive overview of Kant's philosophy and its impact upon philosophy and philosophers. Distinguished Kant specialists provide an up-to-date summary of the results of current research in their fields and give their own take on what they believe are the most significant debates influencing research, drawing original conclusions.

Cambridge Elements

The Philosophy of Immanuel Kant

Elements in the Series

Kant's Late Philosophy of Nature: The Opus postumum
Stephen Howard

Kant on Freedom
Owen Ware

Kant on Self-Control
Marijana Vujošević

Kant on Rational Sympathy
Benjamin Vilhauer

The Moral Foundation of Right
Paul Guyer

The Postulate of Public Right
Patrick Capps and Julian Rivers

Kant on the History and Development of Practical Reason
Olga Lenczewska

Kant's Ideas of Reason
Katharina T. Kraus

Kant on Marriage
Charlotte Sabourin

Kant and Teleology
Thomas Teufel

Kant's Natural Philosophy
Marius Stan

Kant on Social Suffering
Nuria Sánchez Madrid

A full series listing is available at: www.cambridge.org/EPIK

For EU product safety concerns, contact us at Calle de José Abascal, 56–1°, 28003 Madrid, Spain or eugpsr@cambridge.org.

www.ingramcontent.com/pod-product-compliance
Lightning Source LLC
LaVergne TN
LVHW011857060526
838200LV00054B/4382